Man and Money

Man and Money

Keith Ellis

PRIORY PRESS LIMITED

Social History of Science Library

Man the Astronomer *Patrick Moore*
Man the Builder *John Harvey*
Man the Explorer *G R Crone*
Man the Farmer *Robert Trow-Smith*
Man the Navigator *E W Anderson*
Man and the Wheel *D S Benson*
Man the Industrialist *Peter Hobday*
Man the Healer *W R Trotter*
Man the Toolmaker *Michael Grey*
Man and Measurement *Keith Ellis*
Man and Money *Keith Ellis*
Man the Shipbuilder *Maurice Griffiths*
Man the Steelmaker *W K V Gale*
Man the Homemaker *D C Money*
Man the Messenger *Edwin Packer*

SBN 85078 148 5
Copyright © 1973 by Keith Ellis
First published in 1973 by
Priory Press Ltd
101 Grays Inn Rd, London WC1
Text set in Baskerville
and printed in Great Britain by
Page Bros (Norwich) Ltd, Norwich

Contents

1 Why Money?   9

2 Greece and Rome: the Money
  Explosion   29

3 From Iron Bars to Gold Sovereigns   53

4 From Gold and Silver to Paper and
  Brass   75

5 Going Decimal   93

6 Fair Shares for All   103

  Date Chart   123

  Picture Credits   124

  Glossary   125

  For Further Reading   127

  Index   128

List of Illustrations

	on page
Melters in The Royal Mint	frontispiece
The misers	8
American tourists caught in a dollar crisis	10
A mediaeval market	11
American wooden coins	12
African hoe and mat money	13
Malayan tin "tree money"	14
African statuettes used for weighing gold	14
The Abu Simbel temples, Egypt	15
A scribe recording tribute	16
Egyptian trades and occupations	17
Egyptians working gold-containing ore	19
The city of Babylon	20
The tower of Babylon	21
The laws of Hammurabi	23
A Carthaginian decadrachm	24
Coins bearing the heads of Anthony and Cleopatra	25
Coin of Croesus, King of Lydia	26
Chinese money through the ages	28
An Athenian drachma	30
A Syracusan coin celebrating the defeat of Carthage	31
Phoenician traders	31
An Aeginetan coin with tortoise	32
The Greek statesman Solon	33
Coin of Alexander the Great	34
Greek and Etruscan warriors	34
Olympia at its height	35
The Greek statesman and general Pericles	36
A Syracusan silver coin	37
An early Roman bronze "brick"	38
A Roman *as*	39
Roman coins of the Republic	40
A Roman harbour scene	41
Imperial Roman coins	42
The orator Cicero	43
The base of the Antonine column	44–5
An excavated room near Naples	46
Romans at table	48
The Appian Way	49
Statue of Julius Caesar	50
The sack of Rome	52
Early British iron currency bars	53
An early coining die	54
A Celtic copy of a goldstater	55
The landing of Julius Caesar in Britain	55
Coins of Claudius	56
Roman London	57
The first Britannia	58

Treasures from the Sutton Hoo burial 58–9
Saxon and Danish coins 60
The coronation of William the Conqueror 61
Officers receiving and weighing coin 62
"Short cross" and "long cross" Pennies 63
Trading with the Levant 64
Edward III's gold coinage 65
Edward IV's Angel coin 66
A merchant's account book 66
An Exchequer tally stick 67
A religious order settling its accounts 68
A 12th century French moneyer 69
Henry VIII's sovereign 70
Fountains Abbey 71
"The Allegory of Commerce" 72
Longleat House 73
A Tudor company's account book 74
Colonists land in Virginia 76
A tax collector 77
The Stuart mint 78
James I's coinage 79
A 17th century banker 80
William and Mary 81
Bribery: a cartoon 82
A lord mortgages his property 83
A press and dies of George II's mint 84
The first Bank of England note for £100 85
The Bank of England 86
Pitt attacks the Old Lady of Threadneedle St 87
The Capitalist 88
A coining press 89
An American colonial bank note 90
A "Bradbury" of 1914 91
A kite made of paper money 92
The Great Hall of the Bank of England 94
A 19th century US bank note 95
A French bank note of 1792 96
The Royal Mint 98 & 99
A US ½ dollar of 1893 100
A stall after decimal day in England 101
The Tax Gatherer 102
A poor farmyard 104
Newcastle slums, 1880 105
A slum family on the move 106
A London beggar, 1895 107
Victorian London 108
Victorian Brighton 109 & 110
A satirical German coin 111
A Welsh bank note 112
The Stock Exchange 115 & 116
Insurance at Lloyds 117
Finance ministers 118
The US tries to revalue the yen 119
A cheque on a cow 120
The devaluation of the pound 122

1: Why Money?

Money, wrote the socialist playwright George Bernard Shaw, is "the most important thing in the world; and all sound and successful personal and national morality should have this fact for a basis."

It sounds a sweeping statement and one whose truth is not immediately obvious. We all know people who organize their lives with a view to getting as much money as possible. Usually, they do not seem to be happy people. They neglect values which most of us think more important. We know, too, of misers who collect money just to gloat over it, rather than to put it to good use. Bank robbers steal it and sometimes cripple their victims while doing so. Cheats of all kinds trick innocent people out of money they can ill afford to lose. Money can embitter relations between husband and wife, employer and employee, shopkeeper and customer. It does not sound a promising basis for "all sound and successful personal . . . morality."

Nor does it seem to promote "national morality." Nearly every time we open a newspaper we come across reports that show how it has been wasted. We know that in some countries people are starving because they have too little money. Other people have so much that they seem to spend all their time thinking up ever stranger and

Opposite: misers collect money to gloat over rather than to use.

A*

"Tighten your belts, Nixon tells America": young tourists wait outside the American Express offices in London to change money during the 1971 dollar crisis.

more extravagant ways of spending it. Thousands of people have no proper home. Yet property companies build huge office–blocks and allow them to remain empty for years, simply because they can make more money by doing so. Was St. Paul right after all when he wrote, "Love of money is the root of all evil"?

Money also brings problems of its own. In the last half century, it has been the apparent cause of many national and international crises. Inflation hurts us all. Prices continually rise. However hard or conscientiously we work, we find that the promised wage or salary buys less than we expected. Young couples need to borrow money when they wish to buy a home. Yet often they are unable to do so because the building societies have no money to lend. So they have to go on living in unsatisfactory accommodation. As a nation, we seem always to be running into difficulties with our balance of payments. We are selling to other countries less than we buy from them and have to make up the difference out of our reserves. We are like a man living beyond his means who has to keep drawing on his savings to make ends meet. It is a situation that cannot continue indefinitely. Often, too, we see the world's statesmen scurrying from capital to capital in frantic attempts to deal with the latest exchange crisis. Basically, this usually means that one (or more) currency has, in the eyes of the people using it, become worth more, or less, than the official exchange rate. The crisis is usually solved, after a great deal of anxiety and ill-feeling, by re-adjusting the exchange rates to a level agreed by all.

Money is clearly associated with envy, greed, crime, bitterness, social injustice and misunderstanding between nations. But we must be clear about one thing. Money does not *cause* them. In itself it is neither good nor bad. It is just a tool.

Like atomic power, it can be used for our benefit or destruction. We may not have found the best way of using it. But in our civilization, it is hard to see how we could manage without it.

The simple act of buying a pencil, for instance, is much more complicated than we think. We (or our parents) have to obtain the money needed to pay for the pencil. We may work for it, inherit it or receive it in payment for something we sell. Each of these probabilities leads back to an infinity of other arrangements involving our employer's business, our dead relative's livelihood or the finances of the person who bought from us.

When we collect our pencil and hand over the purchase price, the shopkeeper does not keep it all for himself. He sets some of it aside to pay his staff, to settle his rent and rates and to meet his bills for gas, electricity, taxes and other overheads. Most of it goes to the wholesaler who supplied the pencil.

The wholesaler cannot keep all the money. He too has to cover his expenses, not least that of distributing pencils to the retailers who buy from him. The greater part, however, goes to the manufacturer. He too has similar expenses, as

A mediaeval market: every commercial transaction today is linked by money.

well as the cost of the machinery needed to make pencils. He has to buy wood, graphite, paint and other materials. If he wants to sell more pencils than his competitors, he has to spend huge sums advertising them. And so it goes on, a literally endless chain of transactions. Every link is joined to the next by money.

If we think about it carefully, we can see that money serves not just one purpose but several. When our parents set our pocket money at, say, 50p per week, they are doing three different things.

First, they are telling us how much money we shall get. Before they hand over a single penny, we know that we shall get 50p and not 20p or 70p. We can plan in advance how we are going to spend it. We know that we shall find in the shops goods valued in terms of those same pence. We shall be able to buy goods worth 50 of them, no more and no less. It does not matter whether we spend our 50p on sweets or magazines, stamps or a cinema ticket. We are still entitled to the same value. They are worth exactly the same from Land's End to John o' Groat's. Suppose we take our holidays abroad. We can even change our 50p into an equivalent sum of foreign money. (The bank charges us a small percentage or commission for arranging this.) Money, then, is *a standard of value*. It is expressed in pounds and pence as length is expressed in kilometres and metres and weight in kilogrammes and grammes. These units are recognized by everyone.

Secondly, our parents are offering us a choice. Instead of handing over 50p, they could give us, say, a pound of chocolate each week. We should not find this very satisfactory. Even if we liked chocolate to begin with, we should soon tire of so large a quantity. We might prefer a pop record instead. Yet we could not normally go into a shop and exchange our chocolate for one, even if they

Coins have not always been made of metal: a wooden 25-cent piece from Monticello, New York State.

were both of the same value. If we wanted several items from different shops, we should not be able to get them. The shopkeepers would hardly accept loose pieces of chocolate broken from the bar. By giving us 50p in money, our parents avoid these difficulties. They enable us to choose what we want. It can be one item or several. We can exchange our 50p for the same value of goods from almost any country in the world. Money then is also *a medium of exchange*.

Our 50p have yet another advantage. Some weeks, we may not wish to spend them all. Occasionally, we may not wish to spend any of them. So we can set them aside until we need them. Perhaps we plan to buy something expensive. We shall then have to save up for many months or even years. We can do so by taking our money to the bank where it will be kept until we want it. It is hard to think of anything else that could be saved so easily. Certainly not chocolate. Even if we could be sure of exchanging it later for what we wanted, it would be highly inconvenient to have a drawer full of pound bars. They would attract mice. They would melt on a hot day. They would deteriorate through age. They would certainly not be accepted by our bank manager for placing in a deposit account. Money avoids these difficulties. It can conveniently be saved as coins or notes. Or it can be credited to a bank account. It is *a store of wealth*.

The three main uses of money then are as a standard of value, as a medium of exchange, and as a store of wealth. All three are called into play when we buy our pencil. The price, in pence, is an an example of money used as a standard of value. When we place our pence on the counter, money is enabling us to exchange for the pencil our work, our dead relative's possessions or whatever we sold to obtain that money. It is then a medium of

Money has not alway been in coins or notes: *top*, iron hoe money from the Nile, 18th–19th century; and *bottom*, Nigerian mat money, 19th century.

13

exchange. The shopkeeper puts some of the pence aside until he has to pay his various bills. The same money then becomes a store of value.

One other point is worth noticing at this stage. Money, we said, was a tool. If we keep a bundle of notes under the mattress, they are not being used. Suppose we put them in the bank. We have the advantage that they will not be lost or stolen. But the banker also has an advantage. He does not simply put our notes in his safe. He lends them to people who can make use of them: traders, property developers, ordinary people who are short of money. He charges these people a fee for hiring this tool. The fee is called interest and is almost always a proportion of the sum hired, or borrowed. It is reckoned on a yearly basis. The banker passes part of the fee to the people who left their money with him in the first place. Hence, we collect interest on the money in our bank accounts. But it is always *less* than the interest charged by the banker to the people borrowing from him. He may pay depositors 5 per cent, while charging borrowers 12 per cent. The difference is his profit.

Living in a world of banks, insurance companies, building societies and finance houses, we find it hard to imagine that there was a time when money was unknown. Yet it did not exist in the earliest days. Rents and taxes were paid in kind: that is, in the form of goods. In Ancient Egypt, herds were counted by royal officials every two

Above: Malayan tin "tree" money, 19th century; *right,* weights for weighing gold in the form of human figures doing various things, 18th–19th century, from Ashanti, now in Ghana.

years and a proportion of the animals was taken for the king. Craftsmen had to give up a proportion of the articles they made, merchants a proportion of their trading profits.

Land was also taxed. Each *nome* or province was assessed separately and two factors were taken into account. One was the land area, the other was the level to which the Nile had risen that year. Together, these gave a fair indication of the size of the harvest and hence of the amount of tax that landowners could afford. Records were made public to ensure that justice was seen to be done. We can still read the official estimate of the area of each nome on a monument in the chapel of Sesostris III near Karnak. Normal river levels are also given. If the river failed to reach these, the nome had to pay less tax. Anyone could check the level for himself by consulting the nilometers erected on the river at three points to indicate the annual rise and fall of the waters. Landowners then had to pay their share of the nome's taxes in the form of cereals, linen or fruit. Men who did not own land had to give so many hours of work.

The king, who was an all–powerful dictator, ruled the country through an army of officials ranging from military commanders to humble scribes. Since there was no money, they could not be paid in the usual way. But the king fed, clothed and housed them, using the goods he had collected as taxes. Many royal estates were run by stewards who gave part of the produce to the king and kept the rest for themselves. Some became rich. The king would reward senior servants with gifts of gold plate. He would also pay for articles ordered from outside craftsmen with manufactured goods or farm produce. Sometimes a quantity of gold would be given instead, not coins but carefully weighed ornaments or jewellery.

Workmen in the king's service could expect

Egypt became a great civilization and a great empire without the benefit of money as a convenient way to exchange and trade.

An Egyptian scribe recording tribute paid to the Pharaoh as a form of tax.

little but their basic rations. Those who hauled stone from the quarries in the desert to the Nile quays received ten loaves and a third of a jar of beer per month. Foremen each received 200 loaves and 5 jars of beer. Clearly they could not eat twenty times as much as workmen. The extra loaves and beer were used for barter, the main method by which the ancients did their buying and selling.

Barter sounds practical. It has been used in our own day by countries who were short of foreign currency, especially by those of the Communist bloc. Schoolboys barter when they swap comics or pictures of football stars. It was common during World War II in prison camps and in newly conquered countries where the traditional money had lost its value. Refugees would exchange a bar of chocolate for ten cigarettes, a pair of boots for an old bicycle. Early settlers in America obtained wives by barter. The Virginia Company, which brought women over from England, charged 100 pounds of tobacco for them.

In the ancient world, barter was almost universal. Farmers in the outlying provinces of Egypt or Mesopotamia would exchange fruit, corn, vegetables and linen for ivory, spices, precious stones and even cattle offered by the nomads who were always pressing on their borders. In Egypt, we read of a house being sold for a bed and two lengths of cloth. Wall–paintings show a cobbler exchanging a pair of shoes for a cake, and a carpenter offering a wooden casket for some fish. Homer tells of ancient Greeks hurrying down to the quays with cattle and skins so that they could barter them for wine.

It sounds much more exciting than choosing a packet of detergent at the supermarket and paying with a few coins. But it must have been extremely inconvenient. Suppose our shoemaker's wife went down to the market hoping to buy oil, cereal and perhaps wine. She had a basketful of shoes to pay for them. What happened if the food merchants already had all the shoes they needed? Even if they agreed to take the shoes, how did they work out how many were a fair "price"? What happened if the shoes turned out later to be badly made? Wives must have wasted hours finding traders willing to take the goods they had to offer. Every shopping expedition must have been a marathon of haggling. Later there was always the possibility of trouble if either party were dissatisfied with what he had got. Clearly too, buying and selling had to be on a fairly large scale. There was no "small change" to buy smaller quantities.

Men gradually realized that they needed agreed units of value. Shoes, food and every other commodity could then be valued in terms of these.

Various Egyptian activities and trades. Each person paid or was paid in kind.

Barter would be simplified. If it was generally accepted that a pair of sandals was worth x units and a given quantity of oil was also worth x units, there need be no haggling. Also, if the oil merchant did not want sandals, it would be much easier for the shoemaker's wife to exchange them for some other article of equal value which the merchant *did* want and to give him this instead.

What should the standard unit be? Clearly, it had to be something of value for which a use could always be found. Cattle were often favoured and we hear from Homer that bronze armour might be worth nine oxen and a female slave four. Our word "pecuniary" comes from the Latin *pecunia* (money) which is itself derived from *pecus,* meaning cattle. "Fee" is thought to come from *fehu od,* which in Old High German meant "cattle money."

However, an ox is far too big a unit for most purposes. It may be suitable for valuing a ship or a house, but useless when buying a needle or a length of material. Besides, oxen differ among themselves. They may be young and healthy or old and sick. They are not *standard*.

The search for a standard of exchange worried most primitive peoples. Shells were used in many parts of the world. So were beans, peas, dried fish and corn. In colonial America, the standard for court fines was malt or beaver skins. Yet none of these was wholly satisfactory. Most of them were difficult to store. Many deteriorated. Hides could be scarred, shells chipped, corn mouldy. So these too lacked the uniformity which is the essence of a standard.

Most civilized peoples eventually found a type of material free from all these disadvantages: metal. It was durable. It was easy to store. Its purity could be checked. It could be measured precisely by its weight. It could be melted down

and formed into pieces of any size required. There were different kinds of metal and from the earliest times, it was recognized that some were worth more than others. A metal's value depended partly on its beauty when used in ornaments but mainly for its scarcity. Gold scored high on both counts. But for many purposes it was too valuable. The amount of gold needed to buy a fish was so small that it could easily be lost. For goods of medium value, silver was found to be more practical. For the small change of everyday shopping, silver gave way to copper, bronze or even lead.

The change from barter to money took place slowly over thousands of years. By the fourteenth century BC, Egyptian armies fighting in foreign lands took silver to buy horses and other necessities.

Egyptians working ore containing gold.

Trade with other countries was usually in the form of gifts between kings. It often happened that one of the gifts was a quantity of gold. So we could say that imported goods were being paid for in gold. Neighbouring kings unashamedly asked the Pharaoh for gifts of gold and we may suppose that their attitude to Egypt was largely decided by whether their requests were granted. In such cases, the Pharaoh was buying support or subsidizing allies with gold.

In Egypt itself, gold, silver and even coils of copper wire were used as a primitive form of money, though only rarely, for all three metals were in short supply. The Egyptians did, however, have the idea of valuing goods in terms of copper. The main unit was the *deben*. This simplified barter considerably. A farmer selling an ox worth 119 deben would accept in exchange a variety of goods whose combined value came to 119 deben. We

The civilization based on the great city of Babylon partly used a system of money and partly paid or exchanged in kind.

know the value set on many articles, and payment
might be made up as follows:

20 pieces of cloth	50 deben
1 bronze vase	50 deben
1 razor	10 deben
2 knives	6 deben
1 goat	2 deben
8 ducks	1 deben
	119 deben

No money changed hands, only goods. It is worth
noting how the comparative value of goods has
changed. Nowadays, metal is plentiful. Items like
knives and vases are mass–produced. In Ancient
Egypt, metal was scarce and metal goods had to
be made by hand. Therefore they were much more
valuable in relation to livestock.

The famous tower of Babylon.

Further progress towards true money was made in the other great civilization of antiquity, that of Mesopotamia. It arose some 5,000 years ago between the rivers Tigris and Euphrates, mostly in the area covered by present–day Iraq. It was repeatedly invaded. It was often in a state of civil war. At some periods, it was divided into numerous independent cities and states ruled by their own dynasties. Among the peoples who ruled all or part of it were Sumerians, Akkadians, Amorites, Elamites, Babylonians, Cassites, Hittites and Assyrians. It disappeared from history as a separate civilization in 538 BC when the city of Babylon fell to Cyrus the Great, who incorporated it into the Persian Empire.

Documents found at Mari, which was an Amorite capital in Syria in the second millennium BC, show that the king appointed local officials whose job was to collect taxes. These were mostly in kind and as with the Assyrians a thousand years later, we may guess that they were assessed partly on the size of each landholding and partly on rainfall which largely determined the size of the crop. The official himself did not receive a regular salary. He was given a piece of land which he farmed for his personal profit.

Small landowners obtained whatever they needed by bartering their surplus produce. Workmen were often paid in kind. Their master would give them regular rations of food, wine and clothing, which they could use for themselves or for barter. We can work out some of the quantities from documents that still survive. Men who worked for a Mari perfumier received, among other things, $2\frac{1}{2}$ pints of oil a day. This was used instead of edible fats, butter, soap and hair–cream.

The peoples of Mesopotamia were probably the first to understand the usefulness of a standard of value based on metal. They usually preferred

Opposite : the stone pillar on which are cut the laws of Hammurabi, which laid down a scale of fines and fees.

silver. They already had an agreed system of weights. Their table ran:

60 grains	= 1 *shekel*
60 shekels	= 1 *great mina*
60 great minas	= 1 *talent.*

It went up in sixties because their system of writing numbers was based on sixty, as ours is based on ten. It spread throughout the ancient world, partly through conquest, partly through trade. The Phoenicians, a nation of traders who lived mostly in the narrow coastal strip to the north of present–day Israel, made the Mesopotamian units familiar throughout the Mediterranean.

It gradually became the custom to pay for goods and services with an agreed weight of metal, usually silver. Fines and some taxes were also levied in silver. The laws of Hammurabi, an eighteenth–century BC king of Babylon, are inscribed on a stone pillar which we can see in the Louvre in Paris. Many lay down penalties in silver. Anyone who put out the eye of a commoner or broke one of his bones was liable to a fine of one mina of silver. If an ox known to be dangerous gored a gentleman to death, the ox's owner had to pay half a mina of silver. If the victim was a slave, the fine was only a third of a mina of silver.

Hammurabi's laws also laid down a scale of fees for professional services. For a major operation that saved a gentleman's life, a surgeon could charge ten shekels of silver. Commoners, however, could be charged only five shekels of silver and slaves only two shekels of silver. If a gentleman died under the knife, no fee was payable. Instead the surgeon's hand was cut off.

Another set of laws applied to the city of Eshnunna, which lay to the north–east of present–day Baghdad. They too laid down penalties in silver: a mina for biting off a nose or destroying an

A later Carthaginian coin, of about 200 BC. It shows the goddess Tanit or Persephone on one side and the winged horse Pegasus on the other.

eye; two–thirds of a mina for cutting off a finger; and half a mina for biting off an ear, knocking out a tooth or crushing a foot. They also set the prices to be charged for oil, grain, salt and wool, and even for the hire of transport. A wagon, oxen and driver cost a third of a shekel for a whole day.

By Hammurabi's time, too, the idea of interest was widely understood. It was common for farmers to borrow grain, oil, silver or even slaves from the local temple, which acted as a sort of bank. Like modern farmers, they settled their debts, usually in kind, after gathering in the harvest. If they did not pay up on time, they were charged interest. Farmers could also borrow from merchants. If they did so, they had to pay interest from the start. The standard rate was 20% but 25% was commonly charged on silver and $33\frac{1}{3}\%$ on grain.

The Jews also charged interest on loans, as we can see from the many references to usury in the Bible. Usury was not necessarily a crime. It simply meant charging interest on loans. A reasonable rate seems to have been acceptable, and the laws against usury mostly condemned excessive rates. Also, it was forbidden to take interest from the poor or from anyone else who was forced to borrow out of necessity. "If thou lend money to any of my people that is poor by thee," says God in Exodus 22. 25, 26, "thou shalt not be to him as a usurer, nor shalt thou lay upon him usury." However, there was no objection to charging interest on loans to foreigners. "Unto a stranger thou mayest lend upon usury," said Moses (Deuteronomy 23. 20).

The people of the ancient world used other financial devices that most of us think of as modern. Carthage was a Phoenician colony planted on the North African coast in 850 BC. Yet its traders freely used IOUs written on parchment. The Babylonians and Assyrians regularly used bills of exchange. They would pay for goods not with actual silver but with a written instruction to a third party, who owed them money, to pay the agreed weight of silver for them on a specified date. Sometimes interest was added.

In everyday life, we can assume that payment in silver gradually took the place of payment in kind. By the time of Nebuchadnezzar, king of Babylon (604—561 BC), we know that goldsmiths were customarily paid with silver, usually in the form of a strip. When they did their shopping, they cut this strip into smaller pieces to pay for the goods they bought.

A similar process was taking place in Israel. In early biblical times, the Jews used sheep as a standard of value, but by the second millennium BC they were changing over to precious metals, mostly silver. In Genesis, we read that "Abraham weighed to Ephron . . . four hundred shekels of silver." After being stripped of his coat of many colours, Joseph was sold to passing Ishmaelites for "twenty pieces of silver." In the second book of Kings, Naaman presented Gehazi, the dishonest servant of Elisha, with "two talents of silver in two bags, and laid them upon two of his servants; and they bare them before him."

It must be repeated that shekels and talents were not coins or even units of money. They were *weights* of metal, sometimes in the form of rings, sometimes in ingots or even crude lumps. They were inconvenient as a means of exchange. There was no guarantee that a particular ring or ingot weighed what its owner claimed. Every time it was used in trade, it had to be re–weighed to the satisfaction of both parties. Even when the weight had been agreed, there was no guarantee of the metal's purity. When a merchant parted with his frankincense or myrrh, how was he to know that the ingots he had accepted from the departing caravan were solid gold or just iron with gold

In 32 BC an Egyptian coin, a *tetradrachm*, had Cleopatra's head on one side and Anthony's on the other.

coating? Even if a scratch showed that the metal was consistent right through the ingot, how could he be sure that it had not been adulterated with silver or with some other less precious metal?

The Cappadocians saw a glimmering of a solution as early as 2150 BC. They were a sheep–herding people who lived on a high plateau in eastern Asia Minor. When a merchant offered silver in exchange for goods, he stamped it with his seal. The state too sometimes placed its seal on ingots and there is some evidence that these were preferred to those carrying private seals. Scholars do not agree, however, whether a seal was meant to *guarantee* an ingot's weight or purity. Lumps of stamped silver have also been found at Knossos, the centre of the Minoan civilization which flourished in Crete from the fourth millennium to the second millennium BC. The stamps showed their weight, but again we do not know their exact status. Nor do we know who put them on the metal.

That is why the ugly little dumps, or slugs, of electrum circulated in Lydia during the reign of King Gyges (686—652 BC) are so important. Lydia was a small state in western Asia Minor which briefly enjoyed power over its Greek neigh-bours until King Croesus was overthrown by Cyrus the Great of Persia in 546 BC. It owed its influence partly to its position on the trade routes

A Lydian coin (enlarged) of the time of King Croesus. A century earlier Lydia had the first known coins.

between Asia and the Aegean, and partly because of the gold it produced. Most of this gold was found in the river beds and was mixed with silver. This alloy was known as electrum. Dumps made from it were stamped with the royal emblem—the head and shoulders of a lion. Most scholars agree that the stamp was a guarantee, backed by the king's authority. It meant that anyone receiving the dump in exchange for goods or services could be confident that it contained a specified weight of genuine electrum.

These electrum dumps, then, were the first *coins*. For coins are simply pieces of metal stamped by the government for use as money. Nowadays, we should hardly recognize them as the forerunners of the elegantly designed pieces of later years. But they served exactly the same purpose. They were a medium of exchange which did away with the need for barter. A man buying a cow no longer had to take along a collection of livestock and manufactured articles. He took a bag of coins instead. He did not have to argue with the seller about the health or quality of what he was handing over, for the value of the coins was guaranteed by the state.

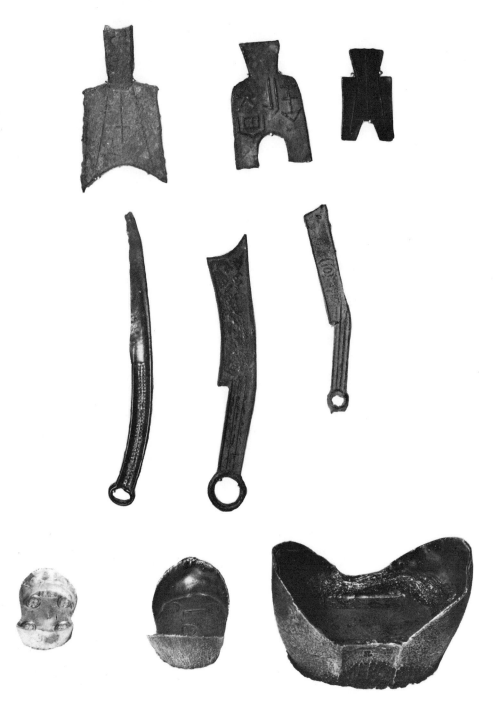

Chinese money: *top*, spade money of Li-chi, 300–200 BC; *centre*, knife money, 1122–1644 AD; *bottom*, boat money, 18th–19th century. The Chinese tended to use representations of practical things for money.

2: Greece and Rome: the Money Explosion

Although there are a few exceptions, such as our current 50p piece, we tend to think that coins should be whole and round. Yet they need not have become so. In northern China, spades were used as a standard of value and even as a medium of exchange. In the seventh century BC, the Chinese made small bronze replicas of spades and agreed that each should have the same value as a real spade when used in trade. Each piece of *pu* or spade money had a hole in the handle so that it could be strung on a cord for easy keeping.

Knives had also been used as a medium of exchange in China. At about the same time as the spade money appeared, we find a second currency in the form of seven–inch scimitar–shaped knives. These too had a hole in the handle. Later, the blade was fined down and the handles became a flat disc with a square hole. Whether or not the first round Chinese coins were simply the handles of knife money without the blade is unclear. But we do know that both spade and knife money were discarded because they were too clumsy for everyday use, and right up till 1900 Chinese coins had a square hole in the middle.

The coins of the Western world are directly descended from the Lydian dumps. They were round from the beginning. They were made by pouring molten metal on to a flat surface where it was allowed to cool. The shape formed was roughly round. Nor did it have a hole in the middle. The only mark was the official seal stamped on the upper side.

If the flat surface used for cooling was scratched, raised impressions of these scratches appeared on the underside of the coin. Some states engraved their seal on the flat surface. The finished coin then had a seal on each side, one raised and one sunk. Various experiments were tried before the type of coin with which we are now familiar became usual. On this, each side bears a different pattern. Both of them are raised.

Those first electrum dumps were the fore-runners of hundreds of different coins that became common throughout the lands bordering the Mediterranean and the Black Sea. They were plentiful because the most favoured metal, silver, was being mined in larged quantities in four main areas of Greece. They were the island of Siphnos in the Aegean, Paeonia in the far north, Laurion near Athens and Thrace in the far north–east.

Some coins were almost works of art. Their weight and purity were checked by priests, whose shrines sometimes acted as banks. It is not sur-

The Athenian drachma showed Athene, goddess of wisdom, and the sacred owl (a symbol of wisdom), an olive branch, and the first letters of the name Athens. Two of these silver coins were the usual day's wage in the late 5th century BC.

prising that coins were often stamped with some religious token. The Aeginetan tortoise and the Eretrian cow–with–calf were both symbols of Aphrodite, the goddess of love. Athens produced a famous series of coins with the head of her patron goddess Athene on one side and Athene's emblem, the owl, on the other.

Mythical or historical incidents were also represented on coins. At Knossos, the well-known story of King Minos was commemorated on a coin showing the Minotaur and a square labyrinth. Selinus, the most westerly Greek settlement in Sicily, was for many years plagued with malaria. When the citizens eventually conquered the disease by draining the nearby swamps, they celebrated their achievement with a coin depicting on one side a river god sacrificing at an altar, and on the other Apollo and Artemis riding in a chariot. After defeating the Carthaginians at the battle of Himera in 480 BC, the Syracusans issued a special coin showing one of their four–horse chariots driving triumphantly over an African lion.

The Syracusan coin minted after the the defeat of the Carthaginians in 480 BC.

Phoenician traders: at one time they had complete control of sea-going trade in the eastern Mediterranean.

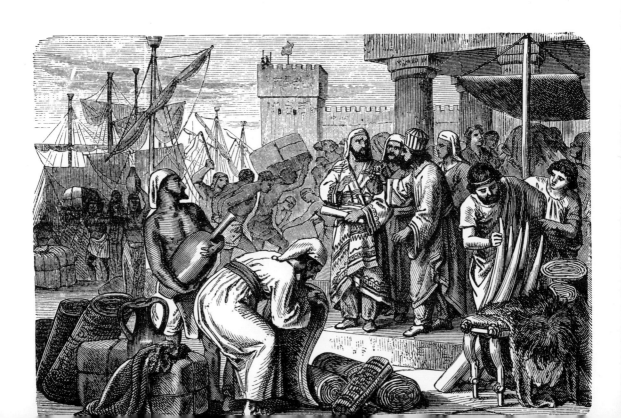

We must remember that the people we know as Ancient Greeks were originally invaders. They were tall, fair, Aryan–speaking peoples who swept down from southern Russia. By 800 BC, they had spread throughout the Greek peninsula and even into western Asia Minor. As they were a primitive people with little civilization of their own, they occupied cities built by their predecessors, a short dark people related to the Egyptians. The Greeks also took over many of their predecessors' ideas and institutions, including their system of weights.

These weights were mainly Babylonian, brought to Greece by the Phoenicians who then monopolized sea–going trade in the eastern Mediterranean. The Greeks adopted the Babylonian talent and its sixtieth part, the mina. But they did not divide the mina into shekels and grains. They divided it into 100 *drachmae,* each consisting of 6 *obols.* Originally, the obol was a tiny iron weight in the shape of a spit or *obolos.* A drachma was literally a "handful" of these.

Greece was not at this time a single, unified nation but a collection of small, independent city states. Each had its own ruler and laws. Some city states issued coins of their own, others used those of their neighbours. Among the most commonly used in Athens were the obol, the drachma and the four–drachma piece, all in silver. There was also a talent of gold and a copper coin equivalent to one eighth of an obol. This was useful as small change for shoppers.

As we have seen, money originally consisted of the weight of metal indicated by the name of the unit. With coins, it was different. The state seal was their guarantee of value. Provided the silver was up to standard and they contained the quantity laid down by law, the name of the coin no longer mattered. A drachma coin no longer contained a drachma's weight of silver, although

The tortoise on this coin from Aegina was a symbol of Aphrodite, the goddess of love.

it still kept the name. Nor did a drachma issued by one state necessarily contain the same amount of silver as that issued by any other state.

In the seventh century BC, the main trading centres of Greece were the cities of Euboea to the east of Athens. Later, the island of Aegina and the city of Corinth, both to the west of Athens, began to outstrip them. The two main currencies used in trade were then those of Aegina and of Euboea. Corinth used Euboea's, Athens that of Aegina.

In 594 BC, Solon was elected archon, or chief magistrate of Athens. Social evils abounded. The poor were heavily in debt to rich landowners. Many had already been sold into slavery. Solon had most of the debts written off. Slavery for debt was abolished. He gave the poor people voting rights and set up popular courts. He stopped the export of corn because merchants were selling it for high prices abroad when there was not enough to feed the people of Athens itself.

He went even further. Athens was no longer friendly with either Aegina or Megara, a neighbouring state which also used the Aeginetan coinage. Solon realized that Athens could not be truly independent unless she had her own money. Like Euboea and Corinth, Athens already had a standard weight or *stater* which was almost identical with the Babylonian shekel. It weighed about 130 grains, compared with the Aeginetan stater of about 185 grains. Solon based the new Athenian money on this lighter stater. A hundred of the new Athenian drachmae were worth about 73 Aeginetan drachmae in terms of silver.

"Devaluation" is a word we frequently hear today. This is precisely what happened to the Athenian currency more than 2,500 years ago. It had several advantages for Athens. It helped debtors especially. They had borrowed the more valuable Aeginetan money. They could now pay

Solon, the radical Greek reformer and lawmaker.

Alexander the Great's head on one of his coins.

it back in the new, less valuable Athenian money. At the same time, Solon was wise enough to make sure that the rich did not suffer. He allowed them to change two of the old coins for three of the new. The state paid for the loss.

These currency reforms greatly helped Athenian trade. They enabled her to break into the new markets being opened up by Corinth in the west. Athens became a great maritime trading nation. Her "owls," as her coins were called, were among the most widely used in Greece. Alexander the Great (356—323 BC), who gave Greece a uniform coinage, based it on the Athenian standard.

Greece became the busiest trading centre in the western world. Her oil, wine and manufactured goods were exported all over the Mediterranean. Yet large–scale industry and banking never developed. It was impossible for individuals, or even groups of individuals, to accumulate enough money to finance them.

This was because Greek city states were not only small but unstable. They rose and fell with bewildering speed. They changed their political systems frequently. In ten years, a single city state consisting of a few thousand citizens might pass from dictatorship, through oligarchy (rule by a few) to democracy. Uncertainty about the future discouraged traders from building up the large sums of capital needed for expansion.

Greek and Etruscan warriors. Military service was compulsory, but soldiers had to supply their own equipment.

The Greeks' attitude to money was another obstacle. In the fifth century BC Athens was a great imperial power. She was also intensely democratic, perhaps more truly democratic than any state before or since. It was generally agreed that no citizen should be prevented from living a full life because he was poor. The wealthy were despised if they flaunted their riches. Alcibiades (450–404 BC), the brilliant but erratic friend of the philosopher Socrates, made himself highly unpopular just by having the walls of his house painted.

Military service was compulsory. Recruits had to supply their own equipment. But here, too, the burden was shared fairly. For the rich tended to serve in the cavalry, the middle classes as heavy–armed troops, the poor as light–armed troops or as oarsmen in the galleys. So the cost of equipment was roughly in proportion to what the individual serviceman could afford. On active service, he was paid a small wage.

The Athenians also made sure that no-one was prevented by poverty from taking part in public life. They did not elect MPs to represent them in their parliament. The city was small enough for everyone to have the right to attend and vote in person. No–one had to worry about losing pay at work. They were paid for attending parliament. State officials were also paid. Judges were chosen

Olympia, at the height of the Ancient Greek civilization.

by lot from a panel on which anyone could enter his name. While serving, they too were paid.

Except in time of war, there were no regular taxes. Most of the state revenue came from customs duties, legal fees and fines, tribute from "allies" and the profits of the publicly owned silver mines. The rich were saddled with huge expenses. It was felt that these would stop them from becoming too powerful. They might be required to equip, maintain and man at their own expense a war galley with a crew of 200. They might have to finance a large deputation to some international festival, organize the distribution of corn or bear the entire cost of putting on a theatrical performance. So they never had large sums for private investment.

Athens was not a socialist state, in any of the modern meanings of the term. Nor was it a welfare state in which the poor and underprivileged are given free handouts by the government and are looked after by an army of state officials. It was simply a body of free citizens who agreed among themselves that money must be kept in its place. Money was not an end in itself, though everyone should make the effort to pay his own way. The opportunity to live a full, well–balanced life and to serve one's fellow men were considered far more important than money–making.

In his speech over the bodies of the Athenian soldiers killed in the Peloponnesian War, the Athenian statesman Pericles (d. 429 BC) summed up the Athenian attitude like this:

Wealth to us is not mere material for vainglory but an opportunity for achievement; and poverty we think it no disgrace to acknowledge but a real degradation to make no effort to overcome. Our citizens attend both to public and private duties and do not allow absorption in their own various affairs to interfere with their knowledge of the city's. We differ from other states in regarding the

The Greek statesman and general Pericles.

man who holds aloof from public life not as 'quiet' but as useless.

On the whole then, money was still seen as a *means*. It made buying and selling easier. It made trade between nations possible on a much larger scale. Ordinary people had more control over their own lives when they were paid in money. They could spend it as and when they wished. A fortunate few were able to visit foreign countries for pleasure, taking with them the cash or letters of credit that would enable them to pay their way. The historian Herodotus (484–424) travelled widely in Greece, Mesopotamia, the Levant, Italy and Egypt. However wealthy he might have been in terms of land or cattle, he could not have moved about the known world so freely without the portable wealth we call money.

(We must remember that the Athenian citizens' attitude to money, though admirable, was possible only because of two separate groups of non-citizens. Slaves, who probably formed a majority of the population, were mostly employed as house-servants and manual workers. They were usually well cared for and adequately paid. They were not segregated socially, could rise to positions of responsibility and sometimes could even buy their freedom. Secondly, Athens had a large group of *metics*, possibly as many as 10,000. These were resident foreigners who had to pay a special tax. They were mostly engaged in trade.)

The Peloponnesian War (431–404 BC) was disastrous for Athens. She lost her empire, her influence and her wealth. Yet in Greece as a whole and in the Greek colonies that fringed the Mediterranean, more money than ever was now circulating. Much of it was gold. Some of it came from temple treasures melted down by the Athenians to help pay for the Peloponnesian War. Most came from mines in Asia Minor and even south Russia.

The head of Arethusa on a silver coin of Syracuse, about 478–450 BC. In Greek legend, Arethusa was a nymph who fled to Syracuse and was changed into a spring to escape her lover.

Previously, Athens had discouraged the use of this gold in order to keep up the value of her silver drachmae. Now she was unable to do so.

The Athenians' attitude to money now began to change. They took it much more seriously. Athenian banks, like those of other states, provided a wide variety of services. They accepted deposits, lent money on security and acted as middlemen between borrowers and outside sources of capital. Some of the larger banks had foreign agents through whom they were able to arrange letters of credit. The growth of industry and trade steadily raised the demand for money. Interest rates went up to 12%, which was then thought to be high.

This new interest in money was the forerunner of what can only be described as a financial explosion. It was set off by an as yet little–known people who lived in central Italy.

Like Greece, Italy was invaded by Aryan–speaking peoples about 1,000 BC. They quickly advanced through the northern and central regions. A group of tribes called Latins settled south of the River Tiber, and a small city state grew up by a ford. This gave it a strategic advant-

An early Roman bar or bronze "brick", struck to commemorate the Battle of Asculum (279 BC) when the elephant corps of Carthage was stampeded by the grunting of pigs, one of which appears on the other side of the bar.

age over its neighbours, whom it quickly dominated. It went on to conquer the Etruscans, a small, dark people of Asiatic origin who had invaded northern Italy after the Aryans. It overthrew the Greek colonies in the south. By 275 BC, it was master of the Italian peninsula as far north as the River Arno. It was, of course, Rome.

In early times the Romans used oxen and sheep as units of value and exchange, with one ox worth ten sheep. They may have used stamped leather as early as the eighth century BC. We know that soldiers and civil servants were paid in salt. Our word "salary" comes from the Latin *salarium* meaning "salt allowance." Possibly salt was used as money.

Like other nations, the Romans understood the advantage of metal money, but they had no gold, and silver was scarce. They settled for bronze or *aes*. Our word "estimate" is thought to be derived from this.

At first, bronze was used in crude lumps which had to be checked and weighed at every transaction. Later, bronze ingots were stamped by the state, probably as a guarantee of purity. But these too had to be reweighed in use and were often cut up into smaller pieces. Finally bronze coins weighing a pound were fully guaranteed by the state. They had to be accepted at face value, even when their weight fell to two ounces, and then to only one ounce after the Punic Wars of the third century BC.

The standard bronze coin, the *as,* steadily lost value as it was successively debased. Merchants preferred to be paid in the old bronze ingots, which were valued according to their weight. They had much more confidence in these than in coins which were worth, as metal, so much less than the value stamped on their face. We can see only too clearly how the true worth of the as

An *as.* The double head of Janus, one of the chief Roman gods, and a ship's prow often appeared on the face of this coin through the ages.

declined over the years when we look at the fines imposed on wealthy criminals. At the beginning of the fifth century BC, a fine of 2,000 asses was thought ruinous. Two hundred years later, the penalty for some offences was fixed at 500,000 asses.

Meanwhile, Rome's trade was increasing rapidly. As her soldiers conquered Italy, her merchants found themselves dealing in grain, cattle, slaves and manufactured articles on a much greater scale than ever before. The as was too small a unit to pay for such large quantities. Moreover, the Romans were now doing business with Greeks in the coastal cities. The Greeks were used to handling silver and thought little of Roman bronze. The outcome was inevitable. In 269 BC the Romans also issued silver coins. The basic unit was the *denarius*, equivalent in weight to a drachma. It was worth 10 asses. The *quinarius* was worth 5 asses and the *sestertius*, or sesterce, was worth $2\frac{1}{2}$. Gold pieces were also struck from time to time.

The expansion of Rome had other effects on the money system. Until the end of the second century BC, all men who owned property were required to serve in the army. They had to provide their own equipment. After 406 BC pay was introduced, but it was never enough to cover the expense of keeping their families and slaves to look after their farms. Too often, they returned from a campaign to find their fields overgrown and their cattle dead. The poor had to borrow from the rich. Rates of interest, fixed by law, were sometimes as low as 5 per cent and sometimes as high as 12. In practice they were very much higher than this. Debtors were often unable to pay. Their land was seized. They themselves might be sold into slavery. The rich got quickly richer, amassing large fortunes and estates. On several occasions, the poor revolted against this exploitation. To

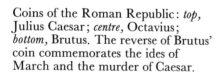

Coins of the Roman Republic: *top*, Julius Caesar; *centre*, Octavius; *bottom*, Brutus. The reverse of Brutus' coin commemorates the ides of March and the murder of Caesar.

restore calm, debts were wiped out by the state or even by the lenders. But the relief was only temporary. The poor soon found themselves in debt again.

Men's attitude to money was undergoing a profound change. The rich no longer thought of it as a means. It became an end. As we shall see, contacts with Greece and the Levant gave the wealthy a taste for luxury on a scale and in a style that has rarely been exceeded anywhere in the world. Yet they used most of their money simply to make more money. Even the very rich borrowed so that they could speculate. There was a boom in property development. Landowners cultivated their land more and more intensively, usually with slave labour. They no longer mainly produced grain. Some ran cattle ranches under farm managers. Others grew olives, wine, fish and even peacocks for the gourmet's table. Usury, graft and extortion were regarded as normal.

At her height Rome was the greatest trading and imperial power the world had ever seen; it was also the first state whose people were obsessed with money.

Coins of the Roman Empire: *top,* Hadrian, who ordered the building of the famous wall; *bottom,* Augustus, formerly Octavius, the first Roman emperor. The month of August is named after him.

Imports of cheap grain from Sicily and North Africa and ruthless competition from the big new farms of Italy ruined most of the small Roman farmers. The citizen army with its property qualification was abolished. An army of long–service paid volunteers took its place. As they were not provided with pensions, they had to rely on bounties or land grants from their generals. This made them more loyal to those generals than to Rome itself. Any general who wished to seize power had a force ready to hand. One result was the series of civil wars that racked Rome, from Sulla's return home in 83 BC to Octavian's defeat of Anthony at Actium in 31 BC.

Loot poured into Italy on an ever–increasing scale. Sulla, Pompey and Caesar all struck gold coins called *aurei* from the gold circulating in Greece and former Greek colonies. Octavius, who became the Emperor Augustus, incorporated *aurei* in the official coinage system in the first century AD. But the most important metal used for coins was now silver. It came mainly from state–owned mines in Spain and Illyria. Usually, these coins showed the head of the emperor on one side and on the other a chariot, the god Janus, or Castor and Pollux. These were all symbols of Rome.

The Roman government had to find large sums to cover its expenses. These included the army, cheap or free corn for the poor, the provision of public games, the upkeep of the state religion and public works such as road–building. But Roman citizens paid few taxes. There was no income tax— only harbour dues, inheritance duty on large estates, a tax of 1% on sales by auction or contract and a tax on the sale of slaves. The rest of the government's income came from its estates in the provinces and from land, property and other taxes levied on conquered peoples.

There was no civil service to collect these foreign taxes. The right to do so was sold at auction to competing joint-stock companies formed by members of the rich, aristocratic equestrian class. These tax-farmers were called publicans. It was up to them to make whatever profit they could. Their agents in the provinces did not always assess taxes fairly. Some were cheats and bullies. That is why they are so often associated with sinners in the New Testament. Similar companies contracted to maintain armies and fleets, build roads and public buildings or arrange for Rome's own supply of corn.

Many of the most influential Romans were investors in these companies. Shares were eagerly sought after. The Forum became a sort of stock exchange. During times of trouble, anxious speculators waited around for news brought by special messenger. Enemy invasion or a crop failure hundreds of miles away might cost them large sums. Naturally, they supported policies which would protect their investments and by extending the boundaries of the empire even further, gave them still greater pickings.

The orator Cicero (106—43 BC) pleaded that the general Pompey should be given special powers against Mithridates, king of Pontus, who was threatening the Romans in Mesopotamia. In his speech *Pro Lege Manilia*, he pointed out:

> The whole system of credit and finance which is carried on here at Rome in the Forum, is inextricably bound up with the revenues of the Asiatic province. If those revenues are destroyed, our whole system of credit will come down with a crash. See that you do not hesitate for a moment to prosecute with all your energies a war by which the glory of the Roman name, the safety of our allies, our most valuable revenues, and the fortunes of innumerable citizens, will be effectually preserved.

Other members of the equestrian class concentrated on banking, money-changing and

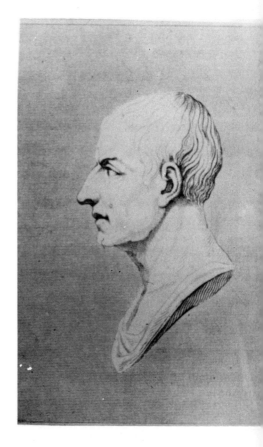

The great writer and orator Cicero.

The base of the Antonine column in Rome celebrates the military might of the Empir

especially moneylending. These too worked mainly from the Forum. They did not simply borrow and lend cash. They arranged complicated deals involving mortgages, bills of exchange and the sale of other people's debts.

Their services were in great demand, especially in the provinces. The publicans were ruthless in forcing local people to pay their taxes on time, even when they had no money. In Asia Minor, the publicans pressed exceptionally hard, raising assessments sixfold in fourteen years. Local kings were sometimes forced to pay excessive levies. Or they might wish to bribe influential officials. If money was lacking for any of these needs, it was borrowed through the Roman moneylenders.

The moneylenders grew ever richer. As we have seen, they had no compunction in seizing the

This excavated room near Naples shows how lavishly rich Romans decorated their houses.

property of debtors who failed to pay. They also charged high rates of interest. In Rome and Italy, 12 per cent per annum was usual. When money was lent in the outlying provinces, there was a greater risk of losing it through enemy invasion or some other unforeseen disaster. To cover this risk, interest rates of 24 and even 48 per cent were commonly charged.

It was not just tax-farmers and moneylenders who exploited subject peoples. Conquering generals carried off gold literally by the ton, and silver in even greater quantities. Little if any of this wealth was used for the benefit of the peoples from whom it had been taken. Most of it stayed in Rome, which then had only a few hundred thousand citizens. The rich were very rich indeed.

The value of money has changed, and is changing, so much that it is meaningless to translate the fortunes of wealthy Romans into modern British pounds. But we can certainly say that this moderate–sized city had many multi–millionaires who lived on a scale which we now associate with Greek shipping tycoons or international film or pop stars. Usually, they had a large house in Rome and a string of other houses in the country or on the coast. Sometimes these were palaces rather than houses.

Many of these wealthy Romans worked hard and spent comparatively little on food, drink or clothes. They enjoyed civilized conversation with friends and studied in their private libraries. Others lived like pigs. They spent many thousands of pounds on a single dinner, stuffing themselves with wild boar, peacocks, thrushes and exotic fish, some of which cost hundreds of pounds each. When they were full, they took an emetic to make them vomit. They could then start eating all over again. They drank prodigiously. For entertainment, they kept their own singers, actors and

Romans at table. Notice the form of lighting and the ornate floor.

dancers, or hired outsiders for the evening. Such banquets sometimes ended in debauchery or fighting. More often, the guests were too drunk and bloated for either.

The general lust for money infected the senatorial class, which came above the equestrian class in Rome's social scale. Its members were mainly employed as state officials, senior army officers and rulers of conquered peoples. Pay was modest. It was often supplemented by bribes and gentlemanly extortion. But most of all, the senatorial class made money by astute investment. They despised professional moneylenders. Yet they lent privately at high rates of interest. Many became very rich indeed. Cicero had a dozen country houses.

Below the equestrian class came a small professional class. Architects, who were mainly

Greeks, were often wealthy. So too were some
doctors. They varied from quacks who spent only
a few months learning their profession to highly
qualified specialists who studied for many years.
Teachers were the lowest paid, especially those in
elementary schools. For the few who became
tutors to aristocratic families, there were rich
pickings. Some became consuls.

The ordinary people scraped a living as best
they could. Many of them had come into the cities
from the country, where most farm jobs were now
done by slaves. The most prosperous were probably small shopkeepers or craftsmen who made
luxury articles for the rich. A good cook could
command a very high salary. Tailors, shoemakers
and bankers might also do reasonably well. The
broad mass of porters, labourers and dockhands,
however, lived precariously. They earned little

The Appian Way at Rome, as it was
during the Empire.

and were liable to lose their jobs if trade slackened. They lived in four–storeyed lodging–houses called islands because they were surrounded by roads. These islands were shoddily built by speculators and often fell down. Fires, too, were frequent. Their inhabitants kept themselves alive mostly on a diet of corn provided free or very cheaply by the state. They drank water from public fountains, eking it out with a little wine.

Their main entertainments were the games provided free by the state. Crowds of up to 150,000 would watch chariot races or, later, contests between gladiators. The senatorial class did not give the ordinary people "bread and circuses" out of charity. They simply feared a revolution. And these demoralizing handouts were about the only benefit derived by the ordinary people from Rome's vast wealth.

The conditions we have been discussing are mainly those of the late republican period. In 23 BC Augustus was given powers which made him virtually dictator. From then on, Rome was not just an Italian city state which had conquered a number of lands overseas. She was now the capital city of an empire that stretched from the Atlantic to the Tigris.

During the next four hundred years the equestrian class lost much of its political power but not its zest for making money. The rich became richer still. Slavery declined and many former slaves were given their freedom. Some of them became millionaires. Instead of setting a good example in sensible living, later emperors seemed determined to outdo their subjects in senseless extravagance.

Nero (37–68), a usurper who murdered his own mother, had his first wife condemned to death and killed his second in a fit of temper, and played dice at many thousands of pounds a point. After the

A statue of Julius Caesar, who was suspected of wanting to make himself Emperor.

fire of Rome, he built himself a Golden House with grounds almost as big as Hyde Park. Domitian, who was murdered by his wife in 96, amused himself by having a naval battle fought on an artificial lake.

Even private citizens spent tens of thousands of pounds on a single carpet. In the fourth century, when the barbarians were hammering at the gates, they feasted on a scale even more lavish than that of Cicero's day. The conditions of the poor deteriorated still further, except that the free "entertainments" now included fights between wild beasts, fights between wild beasts and men, and the tearing apart of bound criminals by wild beasts.

Meanwhile, Roman coins were progressively debased, especially from the beginning of the third century. The denarius, which started as a silver coin, gradually became smaller. More and more copper was added until the proportion of silver was only a quarter. Finally, in the fourth century, coins were minted from an alloy of tin, lead and copper. They had only a coating of silver. Gold coins too were debased and made smaller.

The coinage deteriorated mostly because gold and silver were no longer pouring in from the imperial provinces. Even though public works were largely abandoned, successive emperors could not pay for their extravagances out of income. So they minted inferior money to tide them over.

This made things worse. At home, manufacturers and traders put up their prices because they no longer had faith in the money with which they were paid for their goods. Prices rose by up to eight times in the third century. Foreign merchants trading with Rome refused to take the debased coinage. They insisted on payment by weight of gold or silver. Lack of confidence in the coinage also drove moneylenders to raise their interest rates. These had fallen to 4% under Augustus, the first emperor. By the time of Constantine (272–337), they had climbed back to 36%. In 390, Rome was sacked by the Gauls. The chaotic money system was just one symptom of the general rot that made the final catastrophe inevitable.

The sacking of Rome.

3: From Iron Bars to Gold Sovereigns

We know very little about the money used in Pre–Roman Britain. It seems likely that cattle were the first units of value. It has also been suggested that leather discs were used as a medium of exchange in Scotland and coal discs in Dorset, but the evidence is doubtful. We can be almost sure, however, that there was a currency of iron bars in south–west England. These have been found in Dorset, Gloucestershire, Somerset, Wiltshire and Worcestershire and are shaped like crude sword blades. Although they have lost weight through corrosion, it is believed that they originally weighed about eleven ounces. Some scholars believe that there were smaller units equivalent to a quarter and a half of a standard bar, as well as larger bars weighing twice and four times as much.

A people called the Belgae brought coins to Britain in the first century BC. Crossing over the Channel from their homeland in Gaul, the first wave settled in south–east England between Kent and Hertfordshire, and gradually pushed into Bedfordshire and Buckinghamshire. About 50 BC, a second wave invaded Hampshire and spread as far as Swindon, Devizes, Warminster and Shaftesbury in the west and to Surrey and Sussex in the east.

British iron currency bars are believed to have been the usual medium of exchange before the arrival of the Belgae.

The Belgae were a prosperous, farming people who exported grain to the Continent and brought in oil, wine and pottery. Their coins were originally those of other Gallic tribes. They were poor imitations of the gold staters of Philip of Macedon (382–336 BC) which were widely used in Europe after the Romans seized them in vast quantities in the second century BC. Philip's staters bore the head of Apollo encircled by a laurel wreath on one side and a galloping two–horse chariot on the other.

The Belgae who had settled in England eventually made their own coins. The south–eastern group had mints at Verulamium (St. Albans) and at two other unidentified places, and later at Colchester. The central southern group had a mint at Silchester. They formed their coins in moulds and struck them with a die to give them a pattern. They copied the earlier Gallic imitations of Philip's staters. By now, the original design was almost unrecognizable. The laurel wreath had been formed into a cross decorated with scribbles that were once Apollo's hair and profile. His face had vanished. The chariot also disintegrated and the two horses became one, sometimes with six legs. The metals used were gold, silver and copper.

We must not think that the Ancient Britons were savages. They mined iron and lead. They made ornaments and jewellery of jet, shale, pearls and precious metals. Elegant mirrors have been found. Pottery was widely used, and so were clothes of wool or linen. The Belgic coins clearly proved useful in helping to manufacture and distribute these goods, for three other British kingdoms issued coins on roughly the same pattern. They were the Iceni of East Anglia, the Brigantes who ruled north of the Humber and the Dobuni who spread from Oxford across the Cotswolds to the Welsh border.

After Caesar's abortive invasion of Britain, the standard of coinage improved. It often followed Roman patterns with Roman lettering and heads. Sometimes these were imitations of Augustus' head on Roman coins. Sometimes they were the heads of British kings.

The Roman emperor Claudius finally decided to conquer Britain in 43 AD. It took him four years. From the day his general, Aulus Plautius, landed at Richborough in Kent, the Roman coins clinking in the pouches of the tramping legions were as victorious as their owners. The old British coins lingered on for almost 150 years, especially in the south–west. But the triumph of the Roman currency was inevitable.

Some Roman coins were struck at London, Colchester and elsewhere in Britain but most of these gold aurei, silver denarii and bronze sestertii came from continental mints. There were many different types. They commemorated emperors and their relations, victories and gods. A second–century sestertius of Antoninus Pius celebrated his British campaign with a seated figure of Britannia. She had a spear in her left hand, a

Above: a Celtic copy of Philip of Macedon's gold stater. *Opposite:* an early coining die. The spike on the end was fastened into a wooden handle or block. *Below:* Julius Caesar's invasion of England. He landed near Deal in Kent.

standard in her right and a shield beside her. She was almost certainly the model for the Britannia who appeared on the halfpennies of Charles II fifteen hundred years later. She survived on the penny until the British coinage was decimalized in 1971.

As the barbarians advanced on Italy, Rome's grip on her outlying provinces became weaker and the legions were gradually withdrawn. Some time in the early part of the fifth century, Britain was left to her own devices.

The history of the next five hundred years is confused. We can be sure of little, if anything, about large parts of it. Basically, it is the story of the conquest of Romanized Britons by successive waves of Angles, Saxons, Jutes and Danes. They came to plunder and they stayed to farm. They destroyed the existing civilization. Eventually, they founded another. But it was not until the tenth century that Wessex, Mercia, Northumbria and other independent kingdoms united to form England.

Our knowledge of the coinage of these times is also obscure. It seems likely that Roman coins went out of circulation early in the fifth century and that for the following two hundred years, Britain had no coins of her own. To understand what happened next, we need to look at events in the rest of Europe.

By now, the Western (Roman) Empire had been overrun by barbarians. They set up separate kingdoms and struck coins at a number of mints. Often they used as models coins of the Eastern Empire, whose capital was Constantinople or Byzantium. Shortage of gold, however, forced most of them to standardize on a smaller coin. This was the *tremissis,* which was equal to a third of a *solidus.*

The Franks, who occupied most of present-day France, used gold tremisses. At first, they were

Claudius was fond enough of his mother to put her head on one of his coins.

issued in the name of the king but in the seventh century, bishops and abbeys took over. Finally, tremisses were struck by a thousand separate mints at ports, palaces, fortresses and local capitals. The men in charge of the mints were well–to–do "moneyers" and there were 1,400 of them.

Some of these Frankish tremisses found their way to England. In 1939, an Anglo–Saxon ship was discovered at Sutton Hoo near Woodbridge in Suffolk. It had been buried, perhaps in honour of a local chieftain, towards the end of the seventh century. With it was a hoard of treasure, including bowls, a sword, a helmet and Frankish tremisses. About the same time as the Sutton Hoo ship burial, the Anglo–Saxons were striking coins of their own, possibly at mints in Kent or London.

The shortage of gold became still more acute. Some people think that this happened because the Church was amassing it in the form of plate. In the Kingdom of the Franks, the tremiss gave way to a silver denarius. In England, the Anglo–Saxons issued similar coins called *sceattas*. The word sceatta may have been derived from the Gothic *skatts* meaning first cattle, then wealth. The designs were often based on Roman models but they also

The tiny city of London, as it was in Roman times.

The figure of Britannia on a sestertius Antonius Pius, AD 138–161. The image of Britannia lasted, basically unchanged, on British coins until decimalization 1971.

incorporated Saxon ornaments. The laws of Wessex laid it down that an Anglo–Saxon male was worth 1,200 sceattas but a Briton was worth only 600.

In the second half of the eighth century, the coinage was revolutionized by Offa, king of the Anglian kingdom of Mercia in central England. He introduced a silver coin modelled on the denarius minted in the Kingdom of the Franks by Pepin the Short and spread over Europe by the conquests of his son, Charlemagne. The new coin was thinner, broader and heavier than the sceatta. It appeared in a large number of types, many of them beautifully engraved. It was called a *penny*, a name that has puzzled scholars ever since. We do not know whether it comes from the Latin *pendo* meaning "I weigh," from Penda, an earlier king of Mercia or from some other source. But its significance is not in doubt. It spread throughout

England and became the standard, indeed almost the *only* coin for five hundred hears.

It was well fitted to the needs of the time. At all levels of society, money was used much less than it had been by the Greeks and Romans. Great abbeys and rich lords stored their wealth in the form of personal jewellery and gold plate. Their guests could *see* how rich they were. There were no taxes as such. A lord would pay his dues to the king in kind or by providing men for military service. Men paid their dues to the church by handing over a tithe, or tenth part of their crop. In the villages, rents were usually paid in kind or by doing work for the lord of the manor. Sometimes there was a complicated list of duties that might involve a stint of ploughing at Michaelmas, occasional work in the hayfield or vineyard and a day's harrowing every week. On other manors, the lord would require three whole days every week.

Treasures from the burial at Sutton Hoo. *Opposite:* an enlarged detail from a gold clasp, and *below,* sword fittings made of gold and coloured glass.

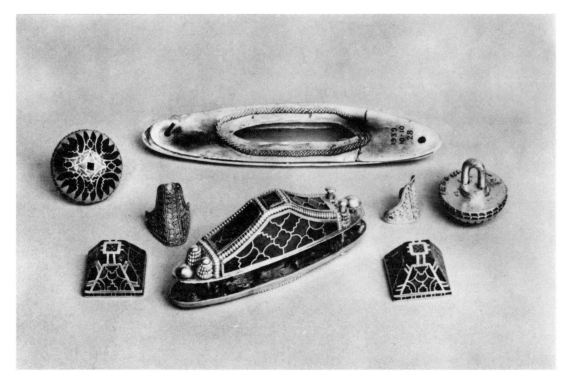

Anglo-Saxon and Danish coins of the reigns of (*top*) Aelfred, (*middle*) Aethelstan, and (*bottom*) Cnut.

Most people lived from day to day. After feeding themselves and their families and paying their dues to their lord and the church, they had little left over. They had no transport to take them to the nearest town which was often beyond walking distance. It is estimated that one person in ten never left his native manor from the day he was born to the day he died. He did not need to. He could buy all the food, clothing and tools he needed in the village.

These cost only a few pence. As late as the thirteenth century at Trumpington, near Cambridge, a man could buy a hoe, a spade, an axe, a billhook, a barrel and two yokes for buckets for only 10d. For hundreds of years, then, the penny was the only coin needed in everyday life. Even when higher–value coins were introduced, the penny survived as small change and is with us even now.

Even though the penny was the only coin in existence, the £.s.d. system of money was already in use. The Franks used for accounting purposes a unit called the solidus and this was worth one twentieth of a pound's weight of silver. (The word pound is derived from *pondus*, the Latin for "weight.") Charlemagne ordered that the value of a denarius should be fixed at one–twelfth of a solidus, thus making a denarius equivalent to 1/240th of a pound. This valuation was accepted for the English penny.

Meanwhile, the shilling had been widely used in England for accounting purposes. It literally meant "a piece sheared off." The first shillings were not coins but lumps of silver cut off ingots or even ornaments and used as money. Its value varied. In some periods, there were as many as sixty to the pound. Eventually, it was established at twenty to the pound, making it equal to the continental solidus. Thus the pounds, shillings and pence system was born and mediaeval book–

keepers gave us the initials £.s.d., standing for *librae, solidi* and *denarii*.

When England was finally united in the tenth century, King Athelstan (924–939) decreed that there should be "one currency." He took away the rights of archbishops and even some bishops and abbots to issue their own coins. Royal control prevented debasement. Even when more pennies were needed, silver was available from the mines of newly conquered Wales.

In some countries coins were not only debased. They were badly worn through use. They were mutilated by "clippers" who sliced bits off them and sold the silver. King Edgar (959–975) devised an ingenious method of raising revenue which also kept up the standard of the currency. Coins were struck at more than sixty mints from Chichester to York, from Crewkerne to Ipswich. This was because of the difficulty of communications. The moneyers, however, had to use official dies for which they were charged high fees. Every three years, Edgar demonetized all existing coins and authorized a new type. The moneyers needed new dies for which they had to pay the usual fee. The system provided the king with a regular income. It also ensured that old coins regularly gave way to new. Under Ethelred the Unready (979–1016), huge quantities of pennies were struck to meet Danegeld, the payments by which it was hoped to buy off the Danes. Vast hoards of them have been found in Scandinavia.

After the Norman Conquest in 1066, William the Conqueror (1066–1087) allowed the monetary

A scene from the coronation of William the Conquerer.

system to continue undisturbed. The only change he made was to raise the silver content of the penny. This made it even more acceptable on the continent where it already had an excellent reputation for its soundness. About this time, too, English currency became known as "sterling." No-one knows where the name came from. One theory is that it meant "little star," because a small star appeared on some of the early Norman pennies.

Under William's successors the coinage began to deteriorate. Worn, clipped and debased coins became so common that people no longer had faith in them. A pound's worth might contain only a handful that were acceptable in trade. Some pennies were cut into two or four pieces to make even more barbarous "halfpennies" and "four-things" (farthings).

In 1124, Henry I tried to reform the coinage. He called in the Bishop of Salisbury who was his Justiciar (roughly equivalent to our Lord Chancellor) and ordered him to call all the moneyers

Officers receiving and weighing coin at the Exchequer, AD 1130–1174. The value of the coin depended on the weight of precious metal in it.

of England to Winchester. They arrived at Christmas. After a searching examination, some were found innocent of debasement and other malpractices and were sent home. Others were fined. The worst offenders had their right hands cut off. "This took twelve days doing," said the Anglo-Saxon Chronicle, "and was good justice, because they had ruined the land with their great quantity of bad money with which they had trafficked."

Henry's attempted reforms were only partly successful and under the chaotic reign of his successor Stephen, things went from bad to worse. Rebellious barons and others issued their own coins. Stephen did not manage to stop them until almost the end of his reign. Credit for restoring confidence in the coinage must go to the next king, Henry II. He cut down the number of mints and stopped the three–yearly changes of coinage. His first crude penny was issued for twenty–three years. In 1180, it was succeeded by the famous "short cross" penny, so–called because it had on one side a cross with short arms. It carried Henry's name but was struck through the reigns of his successors, Richard I and John, until 1247. In that year, Henry III issued his "long cross" pennies. These had the arms of the cross lengthened to make it harder for clippers to cut off pieces of the coin undetected. They lasted until 1279.

There was a good reason for keeping the same design for long periods. The regular changes instituted by Edgar finally had the effect of undermining foreign confidence in English coins. This was especially true in western France where coin designs lasted several reigns. No continental merchant would be pleased to accept large numbers of English pennies towards the end of their life. He would have to change them quickly or risk making a heavy loss. Once they were demonetized,

A crude penny of William I, and the "long cross" which succeeded it in 1247. The arms of the cross were lengthened to make it harder for people to clip the coin's edges.

their value was no longer guaranteed by the English king. Nor, during much of the twelfth century, was there any certainty that they contained as much silver as they should. The result was a sharp decline in trade. Successive English kings hoped to restore confidence, and trade, with their long–lasting types of coin.

England prospered. People had more money to spend. Yet in terms of pennies, the amounts were very small. A town labourer might earn $1\frac{1}{2}$d. a day. For a penny, he could buy a hen or twenty eggs or six cartloads of firewood. The penny was clearly too big a unit for the everyday transactions of

After 1400 European trade expanded rapidly until journeys to the Near East were common. The international standard of exchange was gold.

ordinary people. They needed small change. Edward I (1272–1307) helped them by issuing silver halfpennies and farthings. He also issued a silver groat worth fourpence.

Increase in international trade also encouraged the issue of gold coins. The first, a gold penny, was minted by King Henry III in 1257. The coin was worth twenty silver pence. Here the authorities fell into a trap. They imagined that everyone would agree with the value they set on the coin. But the gold of which it was made was worth, as metal, more than twenty silver pence. Many people made a handsome profit by buying gold pence from the mints at twenty silver pence, melting them down and selling the resulting gold for much more than twenty silver pence. Most of them disappeared.

There was no easy solution to the problem. Even if the relative values of gold and silver coins were exactly equal to the relative values of the metal in them, there was always the chance that the value of one metal might rise against the other. It would then be profitable to buy up these coins and melt them down. When coins of two precious metals were circulating at the same time, it often happened that one or the other went out of circulation because of a change in international metal prices. The only way of overcoming the difficulty was to stop making coins of precious metals and make them simply tokens of value as our present coins are. However, this was several hundred years in the future.

Meanwhile, Edward III made a mistake exactly opposite to that of Henry III. In 1344, he issued florins, valued at six shillings, together with half florins and quarter florins. The gold in them was not worth that much and few people would accept them either at home or abroad. Within months, they had to be withdrawn. Instead, gold nobles,

Edward III's new coins: *top*, the unsuccessful florin of 1344; and *bottom*, the gold noble which replaced it.

c

Above: Edward IV's "angel".

Below: the account book of Gilbert Maghfield, a mediaeval London merchant, listing the money owed to him. The debts which have been paid are crossed out. *Opposite:* A tally stick was used as an official receipt. Notches were cut in the tally to show how much had been paid, then it was split into 2 strips, one for the Exchequer and one for the payer.

half nobles and quarter nobles were issued. There was a good deal of juggling with their weights and also with the weights of new issues of silver pennies, but the noble was widely accepted as worth 6s. 8d. In 1464, further changes in the relative values of gold and silver caused Edward IV to discard nobles and issue three new coins. These were the ryal or rose noble, which had a rose in the centre; the angel, which showed St. Michael and the dragon; and the half angel. Though smaller than the noble, the angel passed for 6s. 8d. and long outlasted the rose noble which was worth 10s.

As we have seen, early mediaeval society was not particularly money–conscious. St. Thomas Aquinas (1226–74), the philosopher and theologian, held that merchants should charge a just price. This would give them a profit sufficient to keep themselves and their families in reasonable comfort according to their station in life. If they made more, they were committing a sin.

Usury, or lending money at interest, was not only a sin but against the law. However, it was agreed that anyone who broke a contract was liable to a penalty. So lenders usually stipulated that the sum borrowed should be paid back almost

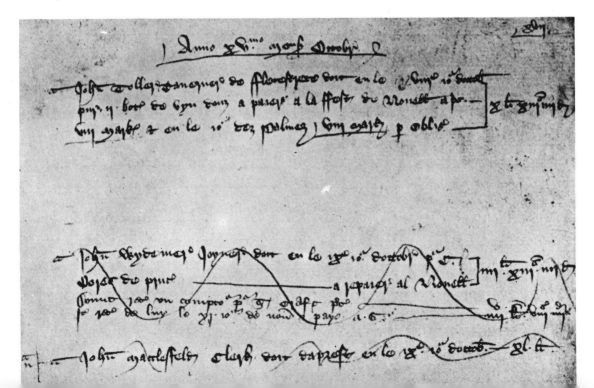

immediately. If it was not, they made a charge, sometimes as high as 5% a month or 60% a year. In theory this was a penalty on the borrower for not paying back the money when it was due. So technically, they were not committing usury. However the system was so silly that it gradually became legal to charge interest from the beginning. Rates then fell sharply.

Men found they had to borrow for all sorts of reasons. Small farmers wished to improve their holdings. A feudal lord needed money for going on crusade. A newly promoted bishop or abbot, even if he had kept a vow of poverty, had to pay in advance a whole year's salary in return for the office. Merchants needed capital to finance trade.

As the variety of needs grew, so did the methods of evading the church and civil laws against usury. Some of these seem to us mere quibbles. Lending at interest was thought sinful because it did not involve any work. But it was decided that risk was morally equivalent to work. So anyone who helped to finance a venture that was in any way risky, for instance a trading voyage to a far country, was entitled to interest on his investment.

The selling of rents was also allowed. In other words, if I owned a piece of land bringing in a rent of £100 a year, I could sign over to you the right to that rent in exchange for a sum of £1,000. You kept on receiving the rent until I bought it back for £1,000. In practice, it meant that I was borrowing £1,000 from you at 10% interest but the fiction of rent charges made it legal. Mortgages too were legal. These were loans, fixed for up to thirty years, on the security of property. As the lender advanced only two–thirds of what the property was worth and could seize the whole of it if the borrower defaulted, mortgages were thought a good investment. Because there was little or no risk, interest rates tended to be about

The Church was the home of great wealth: a religious order settles its accounts.

15%. This compared with between 15 and 50% charged on unsecured loans, depending on the standing of the borrower and the money supply.

In view of their vast wealth, it is not surprising that the great abbeys were among the biggest lenders. Usually, they worked on the basis of a rent charge or mortgage. There is little doubt that they benefited mediaeval agriculture and trade by providing necessary capital. Like the universities, they also made interest–free loans to the poor, though they usually asked for security. On the whole, the monks were good businessmen. They bore in mind the mediaeval dictum "He who practiseth usury goes to hell, and he who practiseth it not, tendeth to destitution."

The Black Death (1348–9) gave money a much more important role in society. It killed off a third of the population, wiping out entire villages. Shortage of labour forced up wages. Many serfs, who had been legally tied to their lord, bought their freedom, or absconded and found work elsewhere. Some landlords turned over arable land to sheep which required less labour. Raw wool was exported to the Low Countries in large quantities.

At the same time, Flemish weavers brought over by Edward III stimulated English cloth–making. Most of the work was done in the country. Merchants sent raw wool by pack horse to village weavers who owned their own looms. The cloth was then collected and put out to other workers for finishing. The merchant needed capital to pay for the wool while it was being turned into cloth. On a much smaller scale, the weaver needed money to pay for his loom. Ports such as London and woollen centres like Colchester thrived. The industry enriched not only town merchants. It brought wealth to wide areas of the country, especially in East Anglia and the Cotswolds.

The break–up of the feudal system and the new

capitalism made England much more money–conscious. In the fifteenth century, Cambridge allowed new mayors 20s. towards the cost of their robes. It paid its members of parliament an allowance of 33s. each session. It spent considerable sums on gifts to the King and influential officials. But not everybody prospered. By the fifteenth century, the population was growing fast again. There was a surplus of labour. Wages fell and many were unable to find work.

We must remember that money still meant coins for the most part. The increasing demand led to a shortage of silver, which was made still worse when many European mines were finally worked out. Some continental countries debased their coins to an alarming degree. Twice in the fifteenth century, England found that her coins were so much more valuable than their continental equivalents that they had to be made smaller to prevent foreigners buying them up and melting them down at a profit.

The situation then changed dramatically. Portuguese navigators opened up new sea and river routes to Senegal and Guinea in West Africa. They brought back gold which was used to finance trade with the East Indies. Portugal rapidly became rich. Meanwhile, new sources of silver had been discovered in the Tyrol, Germany and central Europe. New methods of drainage and of purifying ores led to the reopening of old mines. Finally, Spanish conquests in the New World brought about a flood of gold and later silver that made the Spanish doubloon the most familiar gold coin in Europe.

English coins still kept their reputation for soundness. They were always worth what they were supposed to be worth. Besides, England was gradually moving to a situation we now take for granted. The units we use for accounting (now

A 12th century French moneyer, from a church carving.

Henry VII's sovereign was so called because it showed the king sitting on his throne.

pounds and new pence) have the same names and values as our currency (also pounds and new pence). This was not usual in Renaissance Europe. Even in England, the only coin common to both systems was the penny. Nobles and ryals, angels and groats were the names of coins only. They never appeared in accounts. Also, their value in terms of accounting money was liable to change. Henry VII (1485–1509) brought our coinage much closer to our money of account by issuing the first testoon or shilling. He also issued a double–ryal which became known as a sovereign because it showed the king sitting on his throne. The sovereign was worth 20s. and foreigners soon equated it with the pound sterling.

Under Henry VIII (1509—1547), England caught the money fever that was then sweeping Europe. It was fiercer than any seen since the early days of Rome. The king himself was a victim. He spent money wisely on securing England's position against the Scottish and the French. He also laid the foundations of her future greatness by building a formidable navy and dockyards to maintain it. But he was personally extravagant: he hunted, he held lavish banquets, and his court was one of the most brilliant in history. It attracted poets, scholars and musicians.

Henry quickly spent the wealth accumulated by his father. Also, silver from continental mines found its way into England. The outcome was inevitable. Prices remain steady only when the amount of money in circulation is equal in value to the goods and services that can be bought. If the amount of money goes up or the supply of goods and services gets smaller, prices rise. From the early days of Henry's reign prices started to go up. The cost of food rose by 30%.

Henry tried to get his finances straight by selling off the church lands seized at the dissolution of the

monasteries. He was so desperate that he sold them too cheaply. The speculators who snapped them up made a huge profit by reselling them at their true value.

As a last resort, Henry turned to the coinage. Already, in 1526, he had issued a new set of coins. The silver ones were slightly lighter. The new crown was made of gold slightly less pure than previous gold coins. Though not serious in itself, this debasement was a bad omen for the future. In 1542, he bought a huge quantity of silver and turned it into coins with the same face value as their predecessors but with a fifth less silver in them. He thus made a profit of about 20%. He debased the currency twice more. By the end of his reign, two–thirds of every "silver" coin was copper alloy, a fact that became embarrassingly obvious with use. The effect of numerous fingers

Fountains Abbey in Yorkshire. The monasteries were dissolved in 1536–9, and their huge wealth went to the King and to speculators.

16th century trade: a detail from the "Allegory of Commerce" by Jost Amman.

rubbing his embossed image won him the nickname of "Old Copper–Nose."

Henry made vast sums out of his debasements. The ordinary people suffered. Foreign dealers would not accept them at their face value, so the cost of imports went up. English traders also had little confidence in the new coins. They too put up their prices to match what they thought the coins were really worth. Prices doubled in twenty years.

Confidence was not restored until 1560. The testoons (or shillings) then circulating were divided into two classes. The better ones were declared to have a value of $4\frac{1}{2}$d., the poorer ones of $2\frac{1}{2}$d. On this basis, they could be changed for sound new coins over a period of six months, and were then demonetized. Elizabeth I's profit came to some £50,000. England once more had a currency that inspired confidence. But once more, ordinary people suffered. Prices did not fall. There were no banks in which they could keep their savings. The face value of their tiny hoards was cut by up to 80%.

The flood of precious metals pouring into Europe from the New World continually raised prices.

But inflation was not the only hardship faced by the poor in Tudor times. The population had now reached four million, roughly the level at which it stood before the Black Death. Many no longer had an automatic right to land in return for feudal services to their lord. Yet there were too few jobs to go round, especially when landlords were changing over to sheep.

A minority of peasant farmers owned their land freehold. The rest leased land on various kinds of tenancies. They might have the right to rent it only during their own lifetime. Alternatively, they might have the right to pass it on to their sons on conditions that varied and were often vague.

All tenants were now under fierce pressure from their landlords. Because of inflation, the landlords had to pay higher prices for everything they bought. They used every means possible to raise their tenants' rents. Sometimes, they acted within the law. Sometimes they tricked tenants who were too weak or ignorant to stand up for their rights. It did not matter to the landlords that the tenants were unable to pay increased rents. The new gentry who had grown fat speculating in former monastic lands were keen to buy farms at very high prices. They then had to make the most of their investment, often by changing from arable to sheep.

The new gentry and others who profited from monastic spoils included families who became

Longleat House in Wiltshire: a splendid example of the houses of the new Tudor rich.

The account book of the Woollen Drapers and Tailors Company during the reign of Elizabeth I. The company is now the oldest in Canterbury.

some of the best-known in modern English history. Among them were the Russells and Cecils, the Seymours and the Cavendishes. They kept their estates together by leaving them wholly to the eldest son, rather than dividing them among all their children equally. They built themselves homes ranging from comparatively modest manor houses to palaces like Longleat. They adorned them with tapestries, wood carvings and paintings, paid large sums for miniature paintings and personal jewellery, and dressed elaborately.

Increase in trade benefited town craftsmen and merchants. Freehold farmers also thrived. So did tenants with unbreakable leases. They sold their produce at the new high prices, while paying customary rents that were now absurdly low. Like freeholders, they might build up large holdings. Their descendants were sometimes indistinguishable from the gentry. Others became city merchants. The more successful rose into the aristocracy.

Meanwhile, thousands of former tenants, driven off their farms, were unable to find work on the land. They joined former ploughmen and other unemployed labourers, and often drifted into the towns. Many joined the class of "sturdy beggars" who were the terror of Elizabethan England. Eventually the state provided Poor Relief for the more deserving. But nothing could disguise the fact that the huge amounts of money now circulating in both England and on the Continent had made paupers of those who were unable to take advantage of it.

4: From Gold and Silver to Paper and Brass

From the reign of Elizabeth, England became more money–conscious than ever before. As in ancient Rome, the men who acquired it were not content with enjoying it. They used it to make more. Great trading companies were formed. Some, such as the Merchant Adventurers, consisted of individuals who traded on their own. Others were joint–stock companies. A number of individuals contributed capital for enterprises undertaken by the company as a whole. They shared profits according to the amount of capital they put in. The East India Company and, later, the Hudson's Bay Company were joint–stock companies.

Both kinds of company enjoyed royal charters. They were promised protection against "interlopers." In other words, no other Englishman would be allowed to trade in the territory assigned to them. The government could not, however, guarantee their safety because their operations were too scattered and too distant. Some of them built forts, raised their own armies and had fleets of armed ships to carry their goods. The territories they came to control were to form an important part of the future British Empire. Meanwhile, the people who invested in them often became extremely rich.

Other Englishmen with money to invest formed companies to colonize America. One of the best known was the Virginia Company of London. Shares cost £12.10s. each. The idea was to settle in America those who had failed to prosper in Britain. These included some of the older gentry, former tenant farmers and unemployed craftsmen. They would send back gold and raw materials, and build up a thriving community which would be a rich market for British exports.

The Virginia Company poured hundreds of thousands of pounds into America. But it could not protect settlers against disease or Indians. It could not stop them quarrelling among themselves. It could not stop them concentrating largely on a single valuable crop, tobacco, even when skilled ironworkers, vine–growers and lumbermen were

Late 16th century colonists landing in Virginia. They met unexpected difficulties and the Virginia Company lost money.

sent out to help them diversify. Of this last batch of settlers, originally totalling 4,000, three-quarters died of disease and malnutrition. In 1622, another 300 settlers were massacred by Indians. Two years later, the Virginia Company was dissolved and Virginia became the responsibility of the crown. Investors were finding that it was as easy to lose money as to make it.

During the first half of the seventeenth century, the inflation of the Tudor period continued. It was important politically because both James I and Charles I were caught by rising prices. Unable to meet their expenses, they had to impose fresh taxes; and resentment over these helped to cause the Civil War.

Another cause was the increased importance of money in society. Throughout the Middle Ages, society had been built on a comparatively rigid class structure. Status depended largely on birth. The money relationship, or cash nexus, now became the most important link between man and man. Those who were able to acquire money rose in the social scale. Those who were not tended to fall. To some extent, the Civil War was a contest between the old order and the new. The ancient aristocracy stood behind the king, who claimed to rule by Divine Right. Against him were ranged the new gentry and the city merchants.

In the seventeenth century, too, money itself changed. We must remember that in Elizabethan times it still tended to mean coins of gold and silver. There were no fewer than nine denominations in gold and eleven in silver, some for such odd amounts as three halfpence and three farthings. In the last resort, they were worth whatever value was currently placed on the metal of which they were made. They were crudely manufactured by hammering a piece of metal between two dies. Several strokes were sometimes necessary,

A tax collector argues with members of the public.

Minting coins in Stuart England.

blurring the patterns and squeezing out a "surplus tyre" of metal round the edge. This was a gift for the clippers who could cut it off without spoiling the pattern.

Developments on the Continent brought about an improvement. In the 1540s, German engineers found that much more even, pleasing and legible coins could be made by rolling the metal into sheets, cutting out neat discs by machine and applying the dies by means of a screw press. A Huguenot refugee called Éloi Mestrel tried to introduce this method into England. In 1562, his machines produced excellent sixpences, but Mint officials were jealous and insisted on keeping to the old methods. Mestrel was dismissed. Later, he became a forger and was hanged.

Another Huguenot refugee called Nicolas Briot convinced Charles I that English methods left much to be desired. He had as little success as Mestrel in winning over officials; but in 1661 the Mint yielded to mechanization. The machinery, or mill, was worked by horses. Later, an engraved "collar" placed round each disc during the final process enabled lettering or other marks to appear round the rim. We still have this "milling" on our 5 and 10p pieces. Blind people can tell them by touch from 2p pieces. A further advantage of the new coinage was that the pattern went right to the edge and there was no "surplus tyre" for clippers.

One of the first milled coins was a twenty–shilling piece made of gold from Guinea. It became known as a guinea. In relation to silver, gold increased in value and the guinea changed hands for anything up to 30s. Later, it dropped back to 21s. and stayed there until 1816 when it ceased to exist as a coin. However, the name of guinea continued to be used for a sum of £1.1s. and many professional men charged fees on this basis. It has even survived decimalization. Some payments are still made in "guineas" of £1.05.

The farthing was another seventeenth–century innovation. True, there had previously been a silver farthing but it had been withdrawn by Edward VI because it was too small to handle conveniently. Now there was a greater need than ever for small change. It was met in a way that marked the beginning of a revolution in our coinage: the change from coins that were valuable because of the metal they contained to a purely token money.

James I realized that a farthing of reasonable size could not be made of silver. He therefore decided on brass. There was no suggestion that the new coin should contain a farthing's *worth* of brass; it was to be a *token*. It would have no particular value in itself, and its value depended on its general acceptance as a quarter of a penny.

James I's farthing was a failure. It was thought undignified for the royal mint to handle base metal, so in 1613 the monopoly of making the farthings was assigned to Lord Harington. It was reckoned that 100,000 lbs of brass costing less than £24,500 could be turned into coins with a face value of more than £90,000. Harington was to take a profit of £25,000. The king pocketed the balance as a fee.

Monopolies granted by the king were generally unpopular. The farthings might possibly have been a success if they had been released gradually. But the king could make money only if large numbers were exchanged for coins of gold and silver. The same applied to Harington and other contractors who took over the monopoly. They used every means in their power to persuade people to buy them, offering twenty-one shillings' worth of farthings for every twenty shillings in gold or silver money. The hope of a five per cent profit

James I's currency was the first which bore the words "Great Britain".

A 17th century banker at work.

encouraged traders to buy them for passing on to their customers in change. Unscrupulous manufacturers paid their workmen in farthings.

The situation finally got out of hand when a flood of counterfeits appeared. People accepted them in good faith, only to find them worthless. A law of 1633 ordered that makers of tools for counterfeiting should be pilloried, whipped and fined £100. It had little effect because people who merely owned tools or forged coins were not included. Public confidence continued to wane and the brass farthing became a national scandal. In 1643, the monopoly was cancelled. Owners of genuine farthings were able to redeem them at the expense of the monopoly owners.

The shortage of reliable small change became more pressing than ever, especially after Charles I discontinued the silver halfpenny. Traders took matters into their own hands and minted their own halfpenny or farthing tokens. They were not coins because they were not authorized by the

King, but they were not forgeries either. They were accepted at face value by whoever issued them. This could be a shopkeeper, factory owner, innkeeper, coffee–house proprietor or even a city or town. They circulated freely but not widely. So their usefulness was limited. These seventeenth–century tokens might be round, square, octagonal or heart-shaped. They largely disappeared when Charles II struck copper halfpennies and farthings in the early 1670s. He did not repeat James I's mistake, but issued them from the royal mint.

From Elizabethan times, prices and wages had been controlled, at least partially, by local magistrates. Both were low. Gregory King, a seventeenth–century statistician, estimated that of England's total population of 5 million, 2 million ate meat daily, 2 million twice a week or more and 1 million not more than once a week. These last could not survive without poor relief or some other form of charity. Gregory King reckoned that cottagers and paupers had to manage on an average of £6.10s. *a year*. Labourers and servants who lived out received about twice as much, craftsmen £38, shopkeepers £45 and farmers between £40 and £100. He estimated the average income of gentlemen at £280, knights at £650 and lords at £3200.

Most people spent all their money on food, clothing and other necessities. Even those with a little left over tended to spend it on improving their property or expanding their business. There were no banks, and merchants left their money with goldsmiths for safe keeping. The goldsmiths lent it out at interest and paid depositors up to 6%. Some of the richest families preferred to look after their own money. The Russells kept many thousands of pounds in a trunk at their Strand mansion.

During the eighteenth century, the population

The heads of William and Mary were on their coins together.

rose from under six million to some nine million, mainly because of better living conditions, more abundant food and improved medical knowledge. The northern industrial towns grew rapidly. The population of London almost doubled.

The Industrial Revolution brought a greatly increased demand for copper coins. Factory owners needed them for paying their workers, who needed still more when they came to spend their small wages. The royal mint was unable to keep up with the increased demand. Its machinery was still horse–driven or worked by hand. Nor was there any means of spreading the coins fairly round the country. The more remote manufacturing districts suffered the worst shortages.

Counterfeiters had a field day. Many of them were small Birmingham firms which normally made buttons. They sold their "Brummagems," which were politely called "evasive" coins, at just over half their face value. Large consignments were sent by coach and wagon all over the country. Employers, who were unable to get genuine coins, paid their men with them. It was estimated that between two thirds and three quarters of all the copper coinage in circulation was counterfeit. A

Bribery: a drawing by an 18th century cartoonists. More money in circulation led to more corruption.

18

shortage of silver in the last quarter of the eighteenth century was partly met by over-stamping almost four million Spanish dollars for use in Britain. But silver coins were also forged on a large scale.

Counterfeits were gradually brought under control. But the shortage of copper coins persisted. As in the seventeenth century, the public turned to trade tokens, which did not pretend to be coins and so were not illegal. Now, however, they were often made with steam–powered machinery far in advance of any used by the royal mint. Most were elegantly designed. They showed the name of the issuer and where they could be redeemed. Industrialists often included some recent engineering achievement such as a canal bridge or drop hammer. Many shop tokens carried advertisements such as "The Cheapest Hat Warehouse in the World," "Guests Patent Boots and Shoes" or a gentleman saying "I want to buy some cheap bargains" and his companion replying, "Then go to Niblock's in Bridge Street." Others included such elevating sentiments as "Industry leads to Honour," "Success to the Cider Trade" and "Remember the Debtors in Ilchester Gaol."

By the end of the century, most of the copper in

A young lord borrows money from a moneylender, offering the title deeds of his property as security.

circulation consisted of tokens. The government was forced to take action. Since the royal mint still could not cope, it commissioned a series of twopenny, penny, halfpenny and farthing coins from Boulton and Watt's Soho factory in Birmingham. The twopenny pieces, which weighed two ounces each, were too clumsy for everyday use and were discontinued. The rest were well received.

The problem of distribution remained unsolved. There was so much copper in London that in 1808 the government had to ask Boulton to stop deliveries. Yet there were acute shortages elsewhere. In 1811, a petition from the city of Birmingham to the Privy Council pointed out the evils.

> There are in this town and neighbourhood many thousands of persons whose weekly labour does not produce more than from three to ten shillings, and their employers being compelled to pay several together in pound notes, they are under the necessity of going to public–houses to get change, where, of course, some of the money must be spent to induce the publicans to supply them therewith, or they must buy some articles that they do not want, or in many cases must take the articles of food on credit at an extravagant price, paying for the same when what they have had amounts to a pound.

New copper tokens were minted by the million. Sheffield and Birmingham issued them as poor relief. There were also silver tokens and it was these that finally undermined public confidence. Unlike the copper tokens, they were expected to contain metal worth as much as their face value. Dishonest manufacturers cut the amount of silver in some issues. When this became known, the public refused to accept them. Soon there was uneasiness about the tokens as a whole. The problem was finally solved when Boulton was commissioned to re-equip the royal mint with the most modern steam–operated machinery. In 1817,

A press and dies used in George II's mint.

Parliament passed an Act of Suppression banning "Pieces of Copper and other Metal usually called Tokens," and six years later the last of them went out of circulation.

Meanwhile, an even more important development had taken place. In 1694 the Bank of England was set up. As a method of giving receipts for deposits, it issued bank notes. This was not a new idea, for it had been tried at least four hundred years before by the Chinese and as recently as 1658 by a Swedish bank. The success of the Bank of England issue was due to the promise on the notes that they would be redeemed in full on presentation. Instead of remaining with the original depositor, they passed from hand to hand. Traders accepted them in exchange for goods. The notes thus became money.

They were important because industrialists who wished to expand their businesses needed credit. They had to pay for new factories and equipment. They had to cover the cost of raw materials, wages and other outgoings until the finished goods were sold. The Bank of England could lend money on an unprecedented scale. Its notes carried a

The first Bank of England note for £100. Issued as a receipt for deposits, notes became accepted as currency in their own right.

A view of the Bank of England. The centrepiece was built in 1733.

promise that a particular sum would be paid on demand. As they began to circulate, however, it was clear that people trusted in the promise without testing it out. They circulated just like coins of gold or silver.

The bank quickly realized that it could afford to lend, at a good rate of interest, more money than it had gold. It simply printed notes. If everybody possessing notes had presented them for payment at the same time, the bank would have crashed. But only a small proportion asked for their notes to be changed. So long as the bank had enough gold or silver to cover this proportion it would remain solvent. The proportion would vary from time to time depending on circumstances.

POLITICAL-RAVISHMENT, or 'The Old Lady of Threadneedle-Street in danger!

An 18th century print caricatures the demands for gold made by William Pitt in 1797 on the Bank of England, the "Old Lady of Threadneedle Street", in order to finance the wars against the French.

The Bank of England thrived. In 1751 the government gave it the job of managing the National Debt. It had no rivals, because it was the only joint–stock bank allowed to issue notes. Private banks, many of them set up by merchants or former goldsmiths, were allowed to do so. But their scope was limited because the law required that they had no more than six partners.

There were drawbacks to this arrangement. It meant that many provincial cities were without proper banking facilities because the Bank of England did not trouble to set up local branches. Moreover, the private banks tended to be small. Many were sound but some were tempted to over-stretch their resources. If the public suspected that they were issuing more notes than their reserves warranted, those holding notes rushed to present them for payment. Firstcomers were paid. The rest had to wait until the bank could realize its securities. When these too had been paid out, the bank crashed. Its notes became worthless paper. Anyone who held large quantities of them was ruined. In 1825 sixty–six banks failed in a few weeks. To finance speculation in South America, they had issued too much paper money.

Even the Bank of England faced the danger of a run at times of crisis. In 1696, gold and silver were temporarily in short supply. The goldsmiths tried to put it out of business by buying up as many notes as possible and demanding payment. Luckily, it was able to hold them off long enough to organize a supply of currency. A series of disasters in the Napoleonic Wars forced it to withdraw promise of payment in 1797. At the same time, it increased the number of notes in circulation. Confidence waned, prices rose and paper pounds were soon worth less than gold pounds. At their lowest they were down by more than a quarter. It was not until 1821 that notes could again be redeemed for gold.

The 1825 failures led to a demand for joint–stock banking throughout the country. In 1826, the Bank of England's monopoly was restricted to a radius of 65 miles round London. Other joint–stock banks were allowed to issue notes from offices outside this area. All notes were to have a minimum face value of £5. In 1833, the "country" banks were allowed into the London area. But the Bank of England was given an over–riding advantage. Bank of England notes, unlike those of other banks, were made legal tender. In other words, anyone who was offered them in settlement of a debt had to accept them.

Speculation in the United States followed by a

The Capitalist: "Nothing comes amiss, so money comes with all."

bad harvest led to more monetary crises. Sir Robert Peel was one of many who believed that Britain's money could only be made stable if the issue of notes was more strictly controlled. When he came to power, he persuaded Parliament to pass the Bank Charter Act of 1844. The Bank of England could issue notes in excess of £14,000,000 only if they were fully backed by gold or silver. At the same time, the issue of notes by other banks was restricted to its current level. If they failed or were amalgamated, their right to issue notes would lapse altogether. As expected, these private bank notes gradually disappeared.

The system continued largely unchanged until the First World War. The joint–stock banks thrived. In 1855, the principle of limited liability was introduced for joint–stock companies. Three years later, it was allowed for banks. Under the old system, anyone owning a share in a joint–stock bank was liable to a similar share of its losses. In other words, a man owning 10,000 £1 shares in a bank whose total share capital was £40,000 was responsible for one quarter of any loss. This might run into hundreds of thousands of pounds. His home and all his possessions could be sold to help the bank's creditors. If the bank became a limited liability company, he was liable only to the value of the fully paid shares he owned, that is, £10,000. Naturally, limited liability encouraged many more

Coining presses in the Royal Mint in the 19th century.

A fifteen shilling banknote issued by the Colony of New York in 1775, a year before the Declaration of Independence. With Independence the USA changed over to its present decimal system.

people to invest in banks. They had just as much to gain but very much less to lose.

It might seem that restricting a bank's right to issue notes would reduce its profits. After all, notes were a form of loan on which a bank charged interest. As most of the notes were not backed by reserves, the bank was creating money in order to profit by the interest. But money could be created in other ways too, especially by the use of cheques. It is no coincidence that the use of cheques became much commoner after the Bank Charter Act. They provided industrialists with the capital they needed for expansion and the banks with a new source of profit.

They work like this: suppose an industrialist (or anyone else for that matter) wants a loan of £1,000. The bank manager will ask for security in the form of stocks, shares or a mortgage on the borrower's property. If the borrower fails to repay, the banker can then sell the security to pay off the debt. In this way, the banker cuts his risk to a minimum. He can now set about arranging the loan.

In most cases, he does not hand over £1,000 in currency. He opens an account for the borrower and credits it with £1,000. When the borrower has to meet bills for £1,000, he still does not draw it out in cash. He pays the bills with cheques, which are simply instructions to his bank to pay his creditors from his account. In most cases, his creditors do not want cash either. They pay the cheques into their own bank accounts. Their banks then call on the issuing bank for the sums mentioned on the cheques. But again, little cash is involved. For these cheques are just a few of the millions drawn every day. Instead of paying cash for each one individually, the banks send all the cheques to a clearing house.

Here, all the sums owed by each bank to the rest are set off against the sums owed to it by the rest. Most of the debts and credits cancel out. At the end of the day, the amount of money that has to change hands is very small. Even when we add the sums paid out to their own customers, banks need keep in cash only some eight per cent of the money in their customers' accounts. The rest is created and the interest on it pure profit.

But we must be clear what we mean by "creation." The banker always has security which he can realize if the borrower defaults. We sometimes talk about "unsecured" loans. But really, there are no such things. The security is the borrower's earning power. No banker would give an unsecured loan to someone without a job or other income. He does not, therefore, create money out of nothing. He puts idle assets to work. The amount he can create is limited then by his reserves of currency and by the amount of security available.

In 1914, the government realized that vast sums of money would be needed to finance the war. It decided to issue its own paper currency called treasury notes. These were for £1 and 10s. They were not bank notes but they were used in exactly the same way. They even carried a promise of redemption at the Bank of England. It was against the law either to export gold or to melt it down, so the promise meant little. But it gave the public confidence. Gold sovereigns were taken in by the Bank of England and not reissued. This steadily growing reserve of gold strengthened confidence still further. By 1921, the value of treasury notes in circulation had reached

The treasury notes issued in 1914 were called "Bradburys", after the signature on the note.

91

In the German inflation of the 1920's, money became almost worthless. Here a boy has made a kite out of bank notes.

£367,626,000. Almost a fifth of this sum was covered by gold.

From 1925, treasury notes were freely convertible into gold, provided a minimum of one ounce was taken. As this cost £1,700, ordinary people did not rush to redeem their paper money. In 1928, the Bank of England once more took over sole responsibility for issuing notes in England and Wales. Notes issued by some other banks were, and are, legal tender in other parts of the United Kingdom.

In 1931, Britain abandoned the gold standard. Pound notes were no longer convertible into gold. To this day, they bear the legend "I promise to pay the bearer on demand the sum of one pound." If we take a note to the Bank of England, however, the pound given in exchange will be another note, or a handful of coins.

Like the paper pound, our present–day coins are almost worthless in themselves. They are merely tokens of value. As long ago as 1816, Britain ceased to use silver as a standard for coins. From that date, the weight of metal in silver coins was worth less than their face value. The government guaranteed them as legal tender and gave them a specific value in relation to gold coins. These still contained the amount of gold corresponding to their face value. So the silver coins could be taken on trust.

In 1920, the amount of silver in a "silver" coin was cut by half. From 1947, even these coins were withdrawn. The remaining silver was extracted to help repay in kind a debt of £75 millions' worth of silver owed to the United States. The coins that replaced them were made of cupro–nickel. Our copper coins are made of bronze. So we have a currency based entirely on trust, one that depends for its success not on its intrinsic worth but on public confidence.

5: Going Decimal

We saw earlier that our £.s.d. system was largely
developed by the Franks. It lasted a thousand
years. But it was complicated. If you bought goods
worth £3.3s.7½d., it took quite a bit of concentra-
tion to work out the change from a five pound
note. Nor could a workman earning 7s.3½d. an
hour easily calculate his wages for a 42–hour week.
Every day millions of office workers, bus conduc-
tors, shop assistants and traders of every kind
struggled with awkward sums. Millions of hours
were wasted and expensive mistakes were made.
But what was the alternative?

One possibility was to have a currency consisting of single units. They could be pounds, or
shillings, or pence, or something completely new.
But how big should they be? We commonly spend
a few pence on a newspaper, two or three pounds
on a book, hundreds of pounds on a car and
thousands on a house. Unless we were to use highly
inconvenient fractions for smaller items, the unit
would have to be something like a penny. But a
house worth £10,000 would then be sold for
1,000,000 (new) pence. Most of us would find this
cumbersome. For large sums, we clearly need
large units.

Should there be two units altogether or three?
Researchers found that two was the better choice.

The Great Hall of the Bank of England.

But it was no easy task to decide what the two units should be. First, let us take the relationship between them. The ancient Greeks counted six obols to a drachma, 100 drachmas to a mina and 60 minas to a talent. The old Dutch *rix–dollar* was divided into 48 *stuivers,* and seventeenth–century Denmark struggled along on *skillings,* sixteen of which made a *mark.* There were eight marks to the *corona danica.* As recently as 1925, Albania changed to a now superseded currency in which 40 *qindar* equalled one *lek,* and five leks one *franka.* Even after the war, India reckoned four *pice* to the *anna* and sixteen annas to the *rupee.* It is hard to see any special advantage in having five, six, sixteen, twenty, forty or sixty as a multiplier. There was no reason to think that Britain would benefit from any of them.

However, there is a case for twelve and it has been put forward most eloquently by the duo-decimalists. They argue that twelve is superior to all other basic multipliers because it has more factors. It is divisible by twelve, one, six, two, four and three. So a currency based on multiples of twelve would make more transactions easier than a currency based on any other small number.

A single biological fact overrides this argument. Men are born with ten fingers, not twelve. For this purely arbitrary reason, ten became the basis of our number system. True, some early peoples counted with one hand only and based their system on fives. Others used toes as well as fingers, and had a separate symbol for twenty. But as early as 3,500 BC, the Egyptians used accumulations of finger–shaped symbols much like our 1 for the numbers one to nine, with a separate symbol for 10. This set the pattern of the future.

Surprisingly, the idea of decimal fractions was not thought up until 1585. In that year, Simon Stevin of Bruges explained a system for writing

down tenths, hundredths, thousandths and so on by adding digits to the right of the whole number. But the decimal point never occurred to him. His method of distinguishing the fractions from the whole numbers was so clumsy that his system was little used. It was John Napier (1550–1617), the Scottish mathematician, who thought of using the dot.

Mathematicians seized on decimals as a valuable new tool. They used them to work out interest tables, logarithms and trigonometrical calculations. There was an odd reluctance to use decimals in everyday life. It was clearly easier to convert, say, 1546d. into pounds, shillings and pence when there were ten pence to the shilling and ten shillings to the pound. All you had to do was to move the decimal point one place to the left at each stage. The same was true of other currencies. But men are always suspicious of change, especially where money is involved. The seventeenth century was a time of great uncertainty. Inflation, debasement and clipping all threatened the value of money. No–one wanted to risk the stability that remained by changing the basis of the system.

A 2-dollar note issued by the Baltimore Savings Institute in 1940.

There were two situations, however, in which those objections need not apply: when the existing currency was already in a state of chaos, and after a revolution, when a new currency was being started from scratch. In the United States of America, both situations were present together.

The money system was in confusion. While the individual states had been British colonies, the money of account had been pounds, shillings and pence. The British had never struck any coins for America and the currency with which business was conducted included coins from the mother country, guineas, pistoles, crowns and livres from France, moidores and johannes from Portugal, and dollars, doubloons and pistoles from Spain. By far the most widely used of these coins were Spanish dollars. Their value varied from state to state.

The Americans clearly needed a new money system. They decided it must be decimal. The

A French note for 400 livres issued in 1792, the first year of the Republic, just before the new decimal currency and the invention of the Franc.

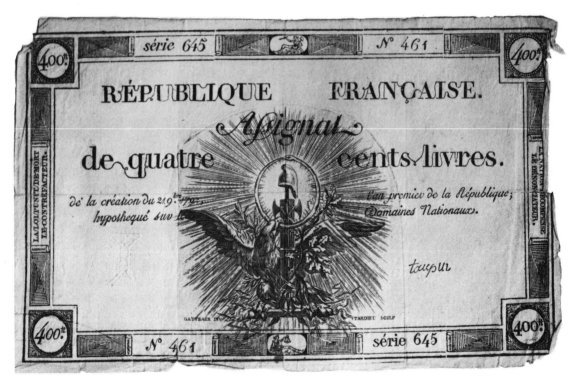

men who had cast off the yoke of the British Empire did not wish to perpetuate its follies. By rejecting pounds, shillings and pence and all the other European systems, they were giving notice that the colonial past was behind them and that they were ushering in a new world dedicated to reason. But what should the units be called?

Thomas Jefferson (1743–1826), who was later to be President, pointed out that the Spanish dollar was already the most widely used unit. He suggested that the new currency should consist of dollars, each divided into a hundred cents. His proposal was accepted. The United States of America became the first country to base both its money of account and its coinage squarely on a decimal system.

Since then, almost every country has followed America's lead. In the New World, former colonies struggling to independence were among the first. In 1847, Colombia adopted a system in which a peso was worth 10 *reales* of 10 *centavos* each. Other decimal converts were Peru (1857), Bolivia (1863) and Ecuador (1884).

In Europe a similar impulse had been gathering momentum. Although France retained her traditional currency for the first few years after the Revolution, a decimal currency based on a new unit called the franc was issued in 1794. It was so obviously superior to its predecessor that the Bourbons made no attempt to change it when they were restored in 1814. Other landmarks in European decimalization were Switzerland in 1798 (as a result of French invasion), Spain in 1848 and Germany in 1871.

The first daring suggestions for a change in Britain were heard at the beginning of the seventeenth century soon after the appearance of an English translation of Simon Stevin's *Decimal Arithmetic*. Some wanted the pound to be kept as

D

One of the Rolling Rooms in the
Royal Mint, 1883.

the basic unit, others favoured a system built on
units of two shillings. In 1696, Sir Christopher
Wren suggested a system based on a new piece
containing an ounce of silver. "We may call this
piece a noble," he wrote. "Divide this ounce into
ten parts (as it was anciently into twenty) . . .
Lower than this, the brass may be divided into
ten parts also . . . So the noble is divided into ten
primes and a hundred seconds, which centesimal
division will be very proper for accounts." But the
proposal fell on deaf ears and for more than a
hundred years, hardly a word was said against
£.s.d.

The adoption of a decimal currency by America
and France was a setback for the British decimalizers. The one was a collection of breakaway
colonies which had deeply humiliated Britain.
The other was a revolutionary junta that had
overthrown established institutions, massacred
the aristocracy and brought twenty years of war
to Europe. No further proposals for decimalization were made until time had healed wounded
pride and a king was safely back on the French
throne.

On February 25, 1824, Sir John Wrottesley
proposed a motion in the House of Commons "to
inquire how far the coin of the realm could be
adapted to a decimal scale." After acknowledging
the need for a stable currency, he said a decimal
scheme was not "visionary" because it had
already proved workable in France and America.
For Britain, he suggested a pound divided into ten
double shillings, each consisting of a hundred
farthings. Pounds would be converted arithmetic-
ally into farthings or farthings into pounds, by
simply adding or subtracting three ciphers to the
right hand. Such a scheme, based on the division
of the pound into 1000 parts or "mils" became
known as a "pound–mil" scheme.

But Wrottesley had only lukewarm support. In the words of Hansard, "he consented not to press the motion to a division, though he trusted that the young members of the House would live to see the principle of his measure carried into effect."

Sir John underestimated his opponents. But he had at least fired the first shot in a campaign that was to be waged on and off for the next 140 years. Other supporters of decimalization pressed their case both in Parliament and in the Press and when the Royal Commission for the Restoration of the Standards of Weight and Measure reported in 1841, they pointed to the "advantage and facility of establishing in the country a decimal system of coinage."

For a time the tide continued to run with the decimalizers. In 1853, the House of Commons appointed a select committee which agreed that a decimal currency would save time in education, calculations and keeping accounts. Errors would be less frequent and it would be easier to compare British prices with foreign. There would be difficulties in converting toll charges, postage stamps, rail fares and customs duties. But experience in the United States and elsewhere showed that these problems could be overcome. The committee found in favour of a pound–mil system.

The decimalizers smelled victory. In 1854 a deputation waited on Mr. Gladstone, then Chancellor of the Exchequer, and demanded that a pound–mil system be adopted immediately.

Mr. Gladstone listened sympathetically. But he was unimpressed. "I cannot doubt," he said, "that a decimal system of coinage would be of immense advantage in monetary transactions . . . but I do not think, when we come to the adoption of a system, that we have obtained sufficient evidence as to the sense and feeling of the country with respect to it."

Machines for cutting out "blanks" in the Royal Mint.

An American half dollar struck in 1893 in commemoration of Columbus.

The decimalizers did not lose heart. In 1855, Mr. W. Brown moved in the House of Commons "that the initiation of the Decimal System by the issue of the florin has been eminently successful and satisfactory; that a further extension of the system will be of public advantage; and that an humble address be presented to Her Majesty praying that she be graciously pleased to complete the decimal scale." There was a long debate, during which government spokesmen repeatedly warned of the dangers of rushing ahead without adequate preparation. The decimalizers won by 135 votes to 56. The mint actually struck specimen coins inscribed "a decimal penny, one tenth of a shilling" and "ten cents one tenth of a shilling." The government then stopped progress by appointing a Royal Commission, which even rejected the basic arguments in favour that had been accepted almost universally.

For 100 years British governments resisted currency reform, despite various attempts by the Dominions, by Industry and in Parliament to change the system. By the 1950's, Britain and the Commonwealth were almost the only non–decimal countries left in the world. Some of the biggest Commonwealth countries had already decided to change. Unless Britain made up her mind quickly, she would find herself alone with £.s.d. On December 1961, Mr. Selwyn Lloyd, the Chancellor of the Exchequer, announced the appointment of a Committee of Inquiry into Decimal Currency. Unlike previous committees of enquiry, it was not to decide *whether* we should go decimal but how, when and how much it would cost.

The Halsbury committee settled down to choosing between four possible systems: the £–cent (the old pound would equal 100 smaller units), the 100–penny (100 old pence would equal a new unit worth 8s. 4d.), the 10s–cent and the 5s–cent. Its main considerations were the possible effect on prices, the possible effect on sterling in world markets, the ease of translating the new currency into £.s.d. during the change-over period, and the possible need to keep the old halfpenny (equivalent to little more than $\frac{1}{5}$ of a new penny).

The arguments were long and involved. The 100–penny and the 5s–cent were discarded fairly quickly, the first because it was insufficiently adaptable, the second because the minor unit was likely to prove too small. Two points finally swayed the committee. With continuing inflation, the minor units in 10s.–cent would eventually become too small. £–cent would admittedly need a half cent to start with, but it could easily be dropped when necessary. At a time of inflation, it seemed illogical that Britain should halve its major unit.

The second point was even more pressing. The committee questioned experts on international

A vegetable stall just after decimalization.

finance. They were unanimous that the £ must be kept because a change to any other unit might endanger the position of sterling on the international money market. "We recommend," concluded Halsbury, "by a majority of four to two, the adoption by the United Kingdom of a £–cent–half system of decimal currency."

It was decided to keep the old name of penny for the new minor unit, though it would be abbreviated to p, not d. The pound remained the pound. The country went decimal on February 1, 1971. It is ironical that the argument considered the most important by Halsbury proved to be no argument at all. In the ten years after 1963, the pound was devalued twice and then floated. Keeping the pound as the major unit seems to have had no effect whatsoever in maintaining international confidence.

The Tax Gatherer: a 19th century drawing.

6: Fair Shares for All

As we have seen throughout this book, money works in many different ways. An abundance usually leads to expansion and rising prices (inflation). Too little may slow down business activity and reduce prices (deflation). It is forever on the move. Like drifting snow, it piles deep in some places, while all around it is spread very thinly indeed. A sudden change of wind scatters the drifts and forms new ones elsewhere. The amount of money we possess and the way we get it determines more than anything else the pattern of our material lives. This has changed dramatically over the last two hundred years.

During the second half of the eighteenth century, big farmers and landowners prospered. They took advantage of new agricultural methods and machinery. Smallholders were unable to compete. Their wives and children had added to the family income by spinning. As more spinning came to be done in the factories, home work was harder to get. Many families gave up their smallholdings and moved into the towns.

The French Wars, which lasted from 1793 to 1815, made things worse. Poor harvests, cheap paper money (see chapter 4) and a population that had risen by fifty per cent in as many years drove up the price of bread. Yet a surplus of

A 19th century farmyard. British agriculture suffered greatly in the last quarter of the century.

labour pushed wages down. In the rapidly expanding factory towns, men, women and young children worked long hours for a pittance. The young sons of London paupers were torn from their families and shipped to Lancashire by the wagonload to be apprenticed in the mills. Many died under the harsh conditions.

By 1815, smallholdings had virtually disappeared. Rising prices had brought the more substantial farmers and landowners bigger profits and higher rents. Hoping to keep the price of wheat both high and steady, they forced a Corn Law through Parliament. This stopped the import of foreign wheat until British wheat reached the high price of 80s. a quarter. Wide variations in the price of wheat led to new laws which substituted sliding scales for a rigid cut–off price.

In 1846, widespread distress led Parliament to yield to the pleas of the Anti–Corn Law League. This was strongly backed by Northern manufacturers. They wanted Free Trade so that they could import raw materials as cheaply as possible and so that their exports of manufactured goods would not be kept out of foreign markets by retaliatory tariffs. They also realized that the level of wages they had to pay their workers was ultimately related to the price of food needed to keep those workers alive. The Corn Laws were repealed. It was a triumph of the manufacturing classes over the landed interest.

In 1875, English agriculture slumped. Cheap American wheat from the mechanized farms of the virgin prairies drove down the price of home–grown wheat. Ten years later, a flood of frozen meat from South America and the Colonies undercut home–grown meat. Townspeople benefited twice over. They got cheaper food; and the money that overseas countries earned by selling it enabled them to buy British manufactures, so providing jobs for British workmen. The main sufferers were small farmers and landowners who concentrated solely on agriculture. Farm labourers simply left the land and sought work in the towns.

It is hard to generalize about working-class earnings in the nineteenth century. On the land, *average* wages bought as much in 1824 as they had done at the beginning of the French Wars. Within this average, there were wide differences. In some parts of the North, farmers had to compete with factory owners for labour, and wages were comparatively high. In areas of the South, there was a surplus of labour and wages were appallingly low. Some farmworkers became so angry that they took to rioting. In 1830, after a demonstration in favour of a minimum wage of 2s. 6d. a day, three ringleaders were hanged and more than four hundred transported to Australia.

The new poor of the Industrial Revolution: a street scene in a Newcastle slum about 1880.

In the "hungry forties" conditions touched bottom, especially in the southern counties. One man, with a wife and five children, earned nine shillings a week. The earnings of his wife and three boys brought in an extra 4s. 9d. Their diet consisted solely of bread and potatoes with a little cheese and butter. Meat of any kind was a rare luxury. Many of these southern families lived on doughy bread and bean porridge which made them chronically ill.

After 1815, industry slumped. War supplies no longer filled the order books. Yet most European countries were now too poor to buy British goods. Demobilized soldiers, Irish immigrants and those who could no longer earn a living from the land flocked to the towns to compete with urban workers. The towns grew rapidly. Manchester more than doubled in size between 1801 and 1831.

Wages fell continuously. By the middle of the century, a London or Newcastle tradesman might receive £1 a week, but 10s. was more usual in the

D*

cotton factories. One of the groups worst hit by the switch to machines was the handloom weavers. Their average wages slumped from 23s. a week in 1805 to a penny an hour. One mill-owner employed only women and children, none of them over 21. He boasted that he paid them only a shilling each a *week*. By the mid-1840's, Britain had one and a half million paupers.

Pauperdom now meant humiliation. In 1795, the Speenhamland system, named after the Berkshire village where it started, gave the poor a cash allowance to keep them and their families alive. Doubtless it encouraged a few idlers to live "on the parish." But even assuming that the majority of those who received it were in genuine need (as they certainly were), it had two bad effects. Unscrupulous employers deliberately paid starvation wages, knowing that the parish would help with a handout. Partly because of this, the poor rate which was levied to pay for it became so high that it threatened to put many farmers out of business.

In 1834 outdoor relief was abolished, except for the old and sick. Others who needed help could

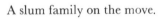

A slum family on the move.

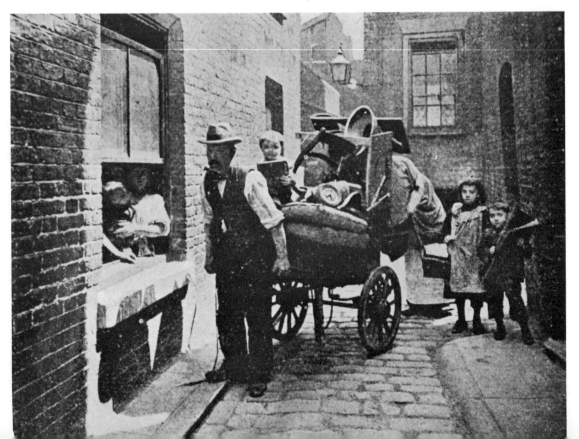

get it only by entering a workhouse. Man and wife were separated to prevent their breeding more children. Conditions were deliberately made harsh to encourage the able–bodied to take jobs outside, even if the wages were miserably low.

After 1846 most workers began to find themselves better off. Free Trade and improved methods of distribution helped to bring down the price of food. A series of Acts from 1802 on had very gradually eliminated the worst evils of child labour. Trades unions became legal. The mindless rioting and machine–breaking of the first half of the century gave way to planned campaigns for higher wages. In Lancashire, the first co–operative brought workers not only lower food prices and a share in the profits, but also practical lessons in democracy and business management.

Yet progress was slow. Lack of money drove thousands of potentially honest young people to crime. London had armies of child pickpockets, prostitutes, fences and coiners. Thousands of others scraped a dubious living as beggars, hawkers or mudlarks, who scavenged jetsam from the Thames mud. The houses run up so quickly in the boom days of the Industrial Revolution were now damp, filthy and dilapidated. In about 1850 some fifty people were found sharing one room measuring 22 feet by 16 feet. As late as the 1890's, 50,000 families in London alone each lived in only a single room.

Yet Britain was not poor. Industry and commerce prospered as never before. We were the most thriving manufacturing country in the world. We were mother country of the biggest Empire since Rome. What happened to the money it produced?

The rich were very rich indeed. Hundreds of successful industrialists entered the peerage, hired architects such as Paxton or Lutyens to build them

A London beggar, 1895. Britain's wealth was greater than ever before, yet there were more poor.

elaborate country houses, and founded families that were soon indistinguishable from those of the traditional aristocracy. The great landowners of the past had leaned heavily on agriculture and farm rents for their prosperity. Yet they too swiftly adapted to the new age. Some made fresh fortunes from coal found under their land. Others drew huge rents from the railway companies whose lines crossed over it, or from the mushrooming towns built in what were once their parks. Many plunged heavily into industry, commerce or banking and showed themselves as able financiers as their forebears had been estate managers.

They lived lives of mediaeval splendour. The Duke of Portland's coal revenues, for example, brought him millions of pounds a year. Besides the usual army of butlers, cooks, valets, maids, porters, stable and maintenance staff, his establishment also ran to a hundred gardeners and roadmen, a stud groom and fifteen assistants for his racing stable, a head greensman and ten helpers for his golf course and even a head instructor and Japanese trainer for his gymnasium. In 1900, a million Britons worked as domestic servants.

The middle classes also took a handsome share of the money made in agriculture and industry. After the French Wars, the National Debt was bigger than ever. Most of it was owed to individual Britons in the form of government stocks on which they drew dividends. There were more than 275,000 "fund holders." The wealthier of them built new houses in the fields surrounding London. These were the first suburbs. They began to visit Brighton by fast coaches which made the journey in a few hours. The men who bought and sold stock for a living were called stock jobbers. Some commuted, living in Brighton but working in the City of London. A quarter of a million of the

Bustling Victorian London: Farringdon Road Station, Metropolitan Railway, 1868.

fund holders collected less than £200 a year in dividends. They were not rich but comfortable and well insulated from the ups and downs of business life.

After 1855, limited liability companies (see chapter 5) offered the prospect of investment with a minimum of effort or risk. Shareholders elected a board of directors who hired professional managers to run the business. The shareholders retired to places like Bournemouth or Eastbourne and lived comfortably on incomes earned, sometimes, at the other side of the world.

The managers were the backbone of a rapidly growing middle class. It included professional men such as doctors, architects, engineers and lawyers who might themselves become extremely wealthy. It also included clerks who spent long hours on high stools writing immaculate copperplate and earning less than higher–paid manual workers. Every large city was rapidly spreading over the surrounding fields. It was mainly the middle

The sea front at Brighton. People began to live here and commute to London to work.

Strolling on the front at Brighton at
the turn of the century.

classes who lived in these new housing developments. Between 1860 and 1900, London's com-
muters increased from 300,000 to 400,000.

After paying for their food, clothes, homes and
usually, too, some form of domestic help, these
middle–class families still had money left over.
They spent it partly in local shops, partly in the
great new department stores which sprang up in
city centres. They subscribed to circulating libraries, musical societies and clubs promoting everything from mountaineering to spiritualism. Religion boomed, especially the social side. Railways
made it possible for Londoners to take day trips
to the south coast and an annual holiday in the
West country. In the North, Blackpool, Llandudno
and even the Isle of Man were becoming popular
resorts with the lower middle and upper working
classes. The more enterprising were already taking
advantage of Thomas Cook's tours to explore
Europe and even Egypt.

It is too early yet to say how money will ultimately shape the twentieth century. But we can
see already that it has been redistributed at a pace
and on a scale never known before. This redistri-
bution has been brought about partly by government policies which have given us old age pensions,
unemployment and sickness benefit, a national
health service and subsidized housing. Death
duties have affected the rich, while income tax
and surtax have sharply cut the take–home pay
of the middle classes. Comparatively, working–
class standards have risen sharply. Even the worst
paid in such industries as agriculture, retail trade
and the health services are much better off than
their predecessors. In the 1930's, deficiency
diseases were still common, and in the industrial
North many working–class children went bare-
foot to school. Poverty of this kind is now extremely
rare. Skilled workmen in many industries can

afford cars, colour televisions and holidays abroad.

The cost of what we buy is affected sharply by the wages paid to the men who make and distribute it. So higher wages have been partly responsible for higher prices and these, in turn, have brought demands for still higher wages. This is undoubtedly one of the main reasons for the inflation that accelerated in the late 1960's and early 1970's, not just in Britain but in many other countries.

It is not the only reason, of course. Growth of credit is another. Before the First World War, few families thought of buying anything until they had saved up the money to pay for it. In the 1920's and 1930's, it became more usual to borrow money so that goods could be used and enjoyed during the time the loan was being repaid. After the Second World War, there was a credit explosion. Although the government restricts credit from time to time, it is usually possible for any man in a steady job to get reasonable credit by a dozen different methods.

Hire-purchase is the most popular. If we buy a car, we are asked to pay a proportion of the cost, usually a third, immediately. This is the deposit. To the rest is added the interest payable for the period of the loan, usually two or three years. The total is divided into twenty–four or thirty–six instalments which we are required to pay monthly. We buy the car only with the last instalment. Legally, the other instalments are hire charges. If we fail to keep them up, the seller may have the right to repossess our car. Until we have paid *all* the instalments, it belongs to him, not to us. We may not sell it without his permission.

Alternatively, we may borrow from a bank. The manager will ask why we want the money and if he is short of funds, he will look more favourably on a request for a loan to improve our property, perhaps by installing central heating, than to spend a weekend in Paris. He will want to be sure

A satirical coin issued in 1923 in Germany, depicting a Nazi riot as a Punch-and-Judy show.

that we can repay the money within a reasonable time. He will also expect us to contribute a proportion of the cost, usually a third, out of our savings. If we can provide security in the form of stocks, shares or the title deeds of our house, he will lend at a lower rate of interest. This is because he is taking less risk. If we fail to repay, he can sell the security and take what we owe him out of the proceeds.

Bank loans are preferable to hire–purchase for three reasons. The rate of interest is lower. It is charged only on the steadily declining sum outstanding, whereas in hire–purchase, it is charged for the whole of the sum originally borrowed for the whole of the period of the loan. Also, interest on bank loans, but not on hire–purchase arrangements, is sometimes allowed against income tax. In other words, you may not have to pay tax on a part of your income equivalent to the amount of interest paid.

Another form of credit is offered by *building societies*. These date back to the eighteenth century. They borrow money from depositors and lend it

This Welsh bank note, issued by "The Black Sheep Company of Wales" in 1969, is not legal tender, but it is claimed that it will be redeemed at face value, like the 18th century trade tokens.

to people who wish to buy houses or flats. Usually, they do not lend the full price of the property but only 90% or less, depending on its age and type. The house buyer has to find the rest from his own resources. The building society takes as security the deeds of the property on the understanding that they will be returned when the loan has been repaid, usually over twenty or thirty years. This arrangement is known as a mortgage. If the borrower fails to repay, the building society can sell the property, take whatever is owing and return the balance to the borrower. Mortgage interest is normally allowed against income tax.

Local authorities and insurance companies sometimes lend money for buying homes. But the great majority of borrowers turn to the building societies. It is the building societies, then, that are mainly responsible for making home ownership possible for millions of middle and working–class families who would otherwise be unable to buy a house of their own.

There are numerous other forms of credit. Shops offer monthly accounts, which have to be settled at the end of the month; budget accounts, which enable the holder to buy goods twelve or even twenty–four times the sum he has promised to pay monthly; and credit sales, in which the item has to be paid for over nine months at most. Anyone who has a life insurance policy on which he has been paying for a number of years (see below) can usually borrow on the strength of it at low rates of interest. Anyone who owns the whole or even part of his house can use it as security for a loan, often at high rates of interest. Check trading is another form of credit. So are credit cards.

These days, people borrow money not just for necessities such as homes or furniture. Sailing boats, flying lessons and winter sports holidays are commonly bought on credit. The amount of out-standing debt in Britain alone runs into tens of thousands of millions. The growing use of credit cards suggests that we may eventually dispense with cash except for small purchases. We shall make most of our payments by signing chits to be debited against deposits that exist only as electrical impulses on computer tapes.

Easy credit has helped to bring about an un-dreamed of improvement in the standard of living. Millions who would never have been able to save up for a car or even a washing machine are happy to buy it on the "never–never", as hire–purchase is sometimes called. Once having got it, they wish to keep it. So they have to keep up the payments. They get into the habit of setting aside a given sum each month and as soon as the first item is paid for, apply a similar sum to buying another. Mass demand sharply reduces costs and so enables us to buy still more goods with our money.

But easy credit is not an unmixed blessing. It contributes to inflation. Many people feel that they ought to have enough money to make sub-stantial hire–purchase repayments *after* buying all the other things they need and want. So they demand, and get, higher wages, which lead to higher prices. The position has been made worse by rising interest rates. Since the early 1950's, demand for credit has grown steadily. So the cost of borrowing has gone up. Hire–purchase borrow-ers commonly have to pay 18 per cent or more per annum. People who borrow on the security of their homes have sometimes to pay as much as 40 per cent. Even building societies, which are non–profit–making organizations, are charging up to $9\frac{1}{2}$ per cent. These high interest rates increase the pressure for higher wages and indirectly raise prices.

The inflation of the last twenty years has brought

about a change in the ordinary person's attitude to saving. When the value of money changed little from decade to decade, most people were content to put their money in the bank at a low rate of interest. They knew that when they drew it out, it would buy roughly the same amount of goods as when they put it in.

This is no longer true. Between February 1950 and February 1973, the value of the pound fell by more than 60 per cent. In other words, a pound drawn out of the bank after 23 years would buy little more than a third of the goods it would originally have bought. Thinking people have therefore turned away from banks for long–term saving. They try to invest their money in such a way that it will maintain or even increase its value in terms of the goods it will buy.

The *stock exchange* is one answer. This is a place where stocks and shares are bought and sold. We cannot go to the stock exchange ourselves. We must ask a stockbroker to do our buying and selling for us. If we are regular customers, we shall have our own stockbroker, just as we have our own doctor or dentist. If we buy or sell only occasionally, we shall ask our bank manager to place an order with the bank's stockbroker. In either case, the stockbroker's commission is the same. We shall also have to pay stamp duty. Stockbrokers rarely, if ever, accept orders for less than £50.

When we buy shares in a company, we hope that it will grow into a bigger and more prosperous company over the years. With luck, the shares that cost us £100 will be worth £400 when we sell them twenty years from now. We hope that this will more than make up for the fall in value of the pound. But there is a snag. The company may do badly. We may find that the shares have gone down, not up. In twenty years' time, they may

The new Stock Exchange building in the City of London.

fetch only £50. As each of those pounds will be worth less than the pounds we invested, we shall have lost twice over.

Investment experts usually manage to avoid losing money in this way. When they think that a company is doing badly, they sell their shares in good time and re-invest the proceeds in a company which they think is doing well. They sometimes make mistakes. Most of the time, they make a profit.

Most of us do not have the knowledge to keep changing our investments. Nor do we think it wise to leave all our money in a single company which may come to grief. Instead, we may put our savings in a *unit trust*. In effect, a unit trust is a fund in which a large number of people buy shares. The managers of the trust are experts in investment and use the money to buy stocks and shares in dozens, perhaps hundreds of companies. They use their professional judgement to switch investments when they think it desirable. The trust charges a fee to cover its expenses. Everything else is shared among the subscribers in proportion to the amount they have contributed. They are paid their share of the dividends collected by the trust from its investments. In theory, the value of those investments could fall and over a short period, often do so. Over a long period, however, the skill of the experts almost always produces a gain. So the shares bought in the trust by subscribers also increase in value.

The two main advantages of unit trusts as a hedge against inflation are that they enable the small investor to spread his money over a large number of shares, thus reducing the risk, and that they give him the benefit of skilled investment management at a low cost.

Life insurance is another method by which ordinary people try to protect the value of their savings. The ordinary type of life insurance is an arrangement by which a person pays a regular sum of money or premium to the insurance company in return for a guaranteed sum when he dies. It is useful as a method of providing for widows and orphans. It does nothing for the insured person while he is still alive.

An *endowment policy* is different. The insured undertakes to pay premiums for a set number of years, perhaps twenty or twenty-five. If he dies during that time, the insurance company agrees to pay out a guaranteed sum. If he does not die, he collects a similar sum at the end of the period. Many people use endowment insurance as a form of saving, especially since it provides protection for their dependents in case of death.

There is one drawback, however. Inflation may cause the value of the guaranteed sum to fall sharply. There are now various schemes for preventing this. Perhaps the commonest is to take

Opposite: on the floor of the Stock Exchange. *Below:* a busy day at Lloyds, the centre of the world's insurance business.

Anthony Barber, Chancellor of the Exchequer in 1970, with John Connally, his American equivalent, as they meet to try and solve another currency crisis.

out a "with profits" endowment policy. The holder usually pays a slightly higher premium. In return, he gets not only a guaranteed sum when the policy matures. He also gets a share in the profits made by the insurance company through investing the premiums of its policy holders. This share may be as large as the sum originally guaranteed. With luck, the total proceeds of a "with profits" policy should more than make up for the effects of inflation.

The falling value of money, then, has significantly changed our traditional methods of saving. The state's need to raise money on a greatly increased scale for social services, defence and other items of expenditure has changed to an even greater degree the scope and nature of taxation.

The *Treasury* is the government department responsible for our national finances. The Prime Minister has the title *First Lord of the Treasury*, but in practice the minister in charge is the *Chancellor of the Exchequer*. It is he who announces the annual *budget* in parliament. After giving a general review of the country's economic position and prospects, he tells us what taxes we shall have to pay in the coming year. He may put taxes on goods imported from other countries to persuade us to buy home–produced goods instead. He may raise the general level of taxation if he thinks too much money is in circulation and is helping to cause inflation. He may lower the general level of taxation at a time of widespread unemployment so that we shall have more money to spend, thus creating a greater demand for goods and therefore more jobs.

Mostly, however, taxes are levied to pay for government expenditure. They take many forms— stamp duty on the transfer of property, excise duty on tobacco and alcoholic drinks, estate duty ("death duty") on the money and property left by people who die, and value added tax (VAT) on many of the things we buy. One of the most important is income tax.

Income tax was levied at the rate of only two old pence in the pound in the 1880's. The rate now is thirty new pence, which is thirty–six times as much. This is some measure of the increased sums spent by the government on our behalf. Income tax is not levied on all our income. We may first deduct allowances for our dependents such as wife and children. There are further allowances for mortgage interest, superannuation payments and numerous other items. Nor do we have to pay it in lump sums, unless we are self–employed. People in most jobs pay it week by week or month by month throughout the year. It is deducted from their pay by their employer who sends it to the Inland Revenue, the government department responsible for collecting it.

Some people think that income tax discourages us from working as hard as we might because we do not reap the full rewards of extra effort. Others believe that it is inflationary. When unions claim a pay rise, they not only have to take into account rises in the cost of living. They also have to think of the extra sum needed to cover income tax. For instance, the cost of living may have gone up by £3 a week but a pay rise of £3 will not be enough to make up for it because of the extra tax that will have to be paid. So the unions have to claim more than £3. As we have seen, prices depend partly on wages. So this puts prices up still more. Despite these disadvantages, however, it is hard to think of a fairer method of taxation.

Taxes directly affect us all. On budget day, millions glue themselves to their radios or televisions to find out whether they will have to pay more, or less, for their sweets and tobacco, their beer and their theatre seats.

The international exchange rate has become a pawn in the world of foreign affairs. Here a Japanese cartoonist equates US attempts to revalue the Japanese yen with the defeat of Japan in 1945, in an adaptation of a famous photograph.

In recent years, the national papers have repeatedly held forth on two other items that affect us just as much, but indirectly. These are the *balance of payments* and *devaluation*.

The balance of payments is the relationship between the money we pay to other countries and the money they pay to us. We have to pay each other for goods, for services such as freight charges, insurance and tourist accommodation, and in interest on money loaned or invested. If we receive more than we pay out, we can hoard the surplus as savings against future requirements. Alternatively, we can lend or invest it abroad. If we pay out more than we receive, however, we must make up the difference from our savings or by borrowing from other countries.

No country can live on its savings indefinitely. Nor can it go on borrowing. Even if it can raise loans, interest charges would make the situation even worse. So a country which regularly has an adverse balance of payments must take steps to put matters right. It may do this by encouraging exports, restricting imports and limiting the amount of money that citizens are allowed to take

A light-hearted comment on the strange laws governing money: a cheque is valid no matter what it is written on, so here the writer A. P. Herbert writes a cheque on a cow. He cashed it at a local bank.

abroad as tourists or emigrants. The most drastic step is devaluation.

Devaluation means that a country reduces the value of its currency in relation to the currencies of other countries. If sterling is devalued, we Britons get less francs, marks and lire for our pounds when we take our holidays abroad. In terms of pounds, everything we buy will cost more. Conversely, foreign tourists in England will get more pounds for their francs, marks and lire. In terms of their own currency, everything they buy in Britain will cost them less.

Devaluation helps the balance of payments because it makes our exports cheaper when sold abroad. Foreigners therefore buy more of them and our earnings are increased. At the same time, we in this country have to pay more for goods imported from abroad. So we buy less of them and choose home–produced goods instead. With receipts up and outgoings down, the balance of payments moves in our favour. With luck, it will go into surplus.

The effects are not necessarily permanent, however. We may insist on buying as many imported goods as before and claim higher wages to pay for the difference. Our own exports will then become more expensive because of increased labour costs. They will be less attractive to foreigners and sales will fall. So we shall be back where we started. This has happened several times in the last few decades. Other countries have also faced difficulties, some of them similar to ours, others rather different.

In Britain itself, there is now a greater equality in the distribution of money than ever before. It is true that there are still some very rich people, though on nothing like the scale of the late nineteenth century. It is also true that inadequate people and particular social groups suffer real poverty. These include some widows, abandoned wives and low–paid workers with large families. But the majority of working–class people have improved their position enormously. Most middle–class people are comfortably off, even though their *relative* standard of living has declined. For most people, the problem of finding enough money to enjoy a decent standard of life has disappeared.

Internationally, however, the scene is far less reassuring. The post–war years have seen an enormous growth in the number and complexity of monetary arrangements between individual countries and between groups of countries. Yet we seem always to be on the brink of crisis. Experts cannot agree on the causes, let alone the possible cures. Clearly, there can be no easy solution because each country is afraid that any concessions it makes may leave it worse off than before. Moreover, the position is not static but constantly changing. But with the experience of several thousand years behind us, it should not be beyond our intelligence to devise a workable system of money one day.

Press headlines on the devaluation of the pound in 1967: will a stable and fair system ever be worked out?

Date Chart

BC

18th century	Hammurabi, king of Babylon, fixes fees and penalties in weights of silver.
7th century	Coinage invented in Lydia.
594	Solon's monetary reforms at Athens.
4th century	Alexander the Great (356–323 B.c.) gives Greece a uniform coinage.
c. 289 (?)	Romans first issue bronze coins.
c. 269	Romans first issue silver coins.
c. 75	Invading Belgae bring first regular coinage to Britain.

AD

43	Roman invaders bring Roman coins to Britain.
3rd–4th century	Roman coinage progressively debased.
7th century	Sutton Hoo ship burial with Frankish tremisses.
8th century	King Offa of Mercia introduces the first silver penny.
10th century	Athelstan (r. 924–939) decrees "one currency" for England.
c. 975	Edgar (r. 959–975) starts triennial change of coinage.
1124	Reform of coinage under Henry I.
1157	Henry II abolishes triennial changes.
1180	"Short cross" penny.
1247	"Long cross" penny.
1257	First gold penny issued under Henry III.
1344	Edward III issues a gold florin.
1504	Henry VII issues the first testoon (shilling).
1526–47	Henry VIII repeatedly debases the coinage.
1560	Elizabeth I reforms the coinage.
1613	Lord Harington coins brass farthings under royal monopoly.
1661	Mint changes over to horse–driven machinery.
1663	The gold guineas issued under Charles II.
1672	Copper halfpennies and farthings issued under Charles II.
1694	Bank of England set up.
1696	Sir Christopher Wren suggests decimal coinage.
1751	Bank of England given the job of managing the National Debt.
1797	Bank of England revokes promise to pay gold for its notes.
1817	Trade tokens suppressed.
1821	Bank of England again redeems notes with gold.
1825	Sixty–six banks fail in a few weeks.
1826	Joint–stock banks allowed to issue notes outside the London area.
1844	Bank Charter Act.
1847	The first decimal coin issued in Britain.
1855	Limited liability introduced for joint–stock companies.
1855	A Royal Commission rejects decimalization.

1858	Principle of limited liability extended to banks.
1868	A Royal Commission rejects the idea of an international currency.
1914	The British government issues treasury notes of £1 and 10s.
1920	A Royal Commission rejects decimalization.
1920	The amount of silver in "silver" coins cut by a half.
1928	The Bank of England takes over the issue of £1 and 10s. notes.
1931	Britain abandons the gold standard: bank notes may no longer be redeemed for gold.
1947	Silver in "silver" coins completely removed.
1951	Hodgson committee on weights and measures legislation recommends decimalization of coinage.
1961	The British government decides on decimalization in principle.
1963	Halsbury Committee recommends decimalization on a £–cent–$\frac{1}{2}$ basis.
1971	Britain goes decimal.

Picture Credits

The author and publishers thank the following for permission to reproduce their pictures on the pages indicated: Keystone Press Agency, *frontispiece*, 10, 92, 111, 119, 122; Mary Evans Picture Library, 8, 16, 31 (bottom), 32, 41, 42, 62, 64, 68, 69, 82, 102, 104; the Mansell Collection, 11, 23, 24, 26, 35, 38, 44–5, 49, 52, 55 (top), 71, 72, 76, 77, 80, 83, 100, 108; Crown Copyright, Central Office of Information, 12, 13, 14, 28; Barnaby's Picture Library, 15, 31, 46, 73, 90, 106, 107, 117; Radio Times Hulton Picture Library, 17, 19, 20, 21, 34 (bottom), 54, 56, 66 (bottom), 67, 74, 78, 85, 88, 89, 95, 96, 98, 99, 105, 109, 110; the British Museum, 25, 34 (top), 40, 58, 59, 63; the Metropolitan Museum of Art, 30; Paul Popper, 33, 36, 37, 39, 43, 50, 55 (bottom), 66 (top), 81, 101; the London Museum, 48, 53, 57, 61; the Bak of England, 86, 87, 94; the Press Association, 112, 118, 120. Other pictures are the property of the Wayland Picture Library.

Glossary

BALANCE OF PAYMENTS. The difference between the total sums entering and leaving a country.

BANK. An establishment for keeping and lending money.

BARTER. A form of trade in which goods are exchanged for other goods, not money.

BILL OF EXCHANGE. A written order to pay a sum of money to a named person on a given date.

BUILDING SOCIETY. An organization that borrows money to lend to members for the purpose of buying or building a house.

BULLION. Gold or silver, usually in the form of bars.

CAPITAL. An accumulation of money or property, especially for business purposes.

CHEQUE. A written order to a bank to pay a named sum to a named person or to the bearer.

COMMISSION. A fee for undertaking certain business transactions, for example selling goods or exchanging money, usually a percentage of the sum involved.

CO-OPERATIVE SOCIETY. An organization of buyers or producers who use their collective power to obtain better terms than they could get as individuals.

COUNTERFEIT. Not genuine.

CREDIT CARD. An identity card enabling the holder to charge goods or services to his account.

DEBASE. To adulterate the metal of a coin.

DECIMALIZATION. The change of a money system to one in which the units are multiples of ten.

DEFLATION. A reduction in the supply of money in relation to the goods and services available.

DEMONETIZE. To take away the value of a coin or note as money.

DEVALUATION. The reduction in the value of a currency in relation to others.

DIE. A raised stamp for embossing coins.

DUMP. A primitive, clumsily made coin.

DUODECIMALS. A system of numbers with a base of twelve.

ELECTRUM. An alloy of gold and silver.

EXCHANGE RATE. The relationship between one currency and another.

FINANCE HOUSE. An institution that lends money at interest.

HIRE PURCHASE. A system of buying on credit. The buyer undertakes to repay the purchase price with interest by regular instalments. He does not own the item until paying the last instalment, the rest being, theoretically, hire charges.

INTEREST. A fee paid for the loan of money, usually a percentage of the sum borrowed.

IOU. ("I owe you") A note acknowledging a debt.

JOINT—STOCK COMPANY. A company whose members subscribe to finance common enterprises. Profits, or losses, are divided in proportion to the shares held.

LEGAL TENDER. Currency that must by law be accepted in payment of debts.

LETTER OF CREDIT. A banker's order to himself or an agent authorizing the person named to draw a specified sum.

LIMITED LIABILITY COMPANY. (Ltd.) A joint-stock company whose members are liable for the company's debts only to the face value of the fully-paid shares they hold.

MINT. A place where money is made.

MONEY. Anything used as a medium of exchange or measure of value.

MONEY OF ACCOUNT. A system of money used when

keeping accounts and not necessarily reflected in the coinage.

MONEYER. Someone who manufactures money.

MORTGAGE. The conditional assignment of property to a creditor as security for a loan.

SECURITY. Something given as a surety for payment of a debt.

SHARE. Part of a company's capital.

STANDARD. The stated amount of metal in a coin.

STERLING. The system of money based on the British pound.

STOCK. (a) The capital of a joint–stock company. (b) Money lent to a government at fixed interest.

TARIFF. Customs duty on imports or exports.

TOKEN. (a) A form of money whose intrinsic value is worth less than its face value, e.g. a 50p piece. (b) (Historical) A piece of metal without government backing used as money and guaranteed by the trader, bank, corporation or other body which issued it.

USURY. The practice of lending money at interest, usually high.

For Further Reading

Margaret E. Bowman, *Romance in Arithmetic* (University of London Press, 1950).

Geoffrey Crowther, *An Outline of Money* (Nelson, 1948).

Paul Einzig, *Primitive Money* (Eyre, 1949).

Charles Oman, *The Coinage of England* (Oxford, 1931).

John Porteous, *Coins in History* (Weidenfeld, 1969).

G. W. Southgate, *English Economic History* (Dent, 1970).

J. R. S. Whiting, *Trade Tokens* (David and Charles, 1971).

Index

America, United States of, 17, 18, 76, 88, 90, 92, 96, 97, 98, 99, 104
As, 39, 40
Athens, 30, 31, 33, 34, 35, 36, 37, 38
Augustus, 40, 42, 50, 52, 55

Babylon, 21, 22, 23, 24, 25
Balance of payments, 120
Bank Charter Act, 89, 90
Bank-notes, 85, 86, 87, 88, 89, 90, 91, 92
Bank of England, 85, 86, 87, 88, 89, 91, 92, 94
Belgae, 53, 54
Bible, 24, 25, 43
Birmingham, 82, 84
Black Death, 68, 73
Brighton, 108, 109
Britannia, 55, 56, 57
Building Societies, 112, 113, 114

Carthage, 24, 31, 38
Charlemagne, 58, 60
Charles I, 77, 78, 80, 81
Cheques, 90, 120
China, 28, 29, 85
Cicero, 43, 48, 51
Colchester, 54, 55, 68
Corinth, 33, 34
Credit cards, 113, 114

Debasement, 51, 69, 71, 72
Deben, 20
Decimal currency, 93–101
Denarius, 40, 51, 55, 61
Devaluation, 102, 120, 121, 122
Dollar, 95, 97, 98
Drachma, 32, 33, 94

Egypt, 14, 15, 16, 17, 19, 20, 21, 25, 32, 37, 94, 110

Electrum, 27, 30
Elizabeth I, 72, 74, 75, 77

Farthing, 79, 80, 81, 98
France, 56, 57, 63, 69, 87, 96, 97, 98
Free Trade, 104, 107

Germany, 69, 78, 92, 97, 111
Gladstone, William Ewart, 99
Greece, the Greeks, 17, 26, 30, 31, 32, 33, 34, 35, 37, 39, 40, 41, 49, 53, 59, 94
Guinea, 69, 78, 79

Halsbury Committee, 100–2
Hammurabi, 23, 24
Henry I, 62, 63
Henry VIII, 70, 71, 72
Hire purchase, 111, 112, 114

Income tax, 119
Inland Revenue, 119
Insurance, 113, 116, 117, 118
Interest, 24, 38, 40, 47, 52, 64, 67, 68, 81, 86, 111, 112, 113, 114
Italy, 37, 38, 39, 40, 42, 47, 56

James I, 77, 79
Joint-stock companies, 75, 89
Julius Caesar, 40, 42, 50, 55

Karnak, 15
Knossos, 26, 31

Limited liability companies, 89, 109
Lloyd, Selwyn, 100
London, 55, 57, 68, 82, 88, 104, 105, 107, 108, 110
Lydia, 26, 29

Mesopotamia, 17, 22, 37, 43
Mestrel, Éloi, 78
Mortgages, 67, 113

Napier, John, 95
National Debt, 87, 108
Nile, 13, 15, 16

Obol, 32, 94

Penny, 58, 60, 61, 62, 63, 64, 65, 66, 70, 95, 96, 97, 100
Phoenicians, 23, 24, 31, 32
Poor relief, 74, 106
Pound, 60, 62, 70, 84, 88, 92, 95, 96, 97, 98, 100, 102, 121
Pound–mil scheme, 98, 99

Rome, 39, 40, 41, 42, 43, 44, 45, 46, 47, 48, 49, 50, 51, 52, 56, 58, 59, 70, 75, 107

Scotland, 53, 95
Shekel, 23, 24, 25, 33
Shilling, 60, 65, 84, 95, 96, 97, 98, 100
Solidus, 56, 60, 61
Solon, 33, 34
Sovereign, 70, 91
Spain, 42, 83, 96, 97
Stater, 33, 54, 55
Stevin, Simon, 94, 97
Stock Exchange, 115
Sutton Hoo burial, 57, 59

Talent, 23, 25, 32, 94
Token, 79, 80, 81, 84, 92
Treasury, 118
Treasury notes, 91, 92

Unit trust, 116
Usury, 24, 66

Wales, 61, 92, 112